JAMES BECKWOURTH

LEGENDARY MOUNTAIN MAN

Ann S. Manheimer

Twenty-First Century Books/Minneapolis

To those who blaze paths of all kinds, easing the way for the rest of us

Acknowledgments: My special thanks to Betty Folchi, director of the Beckwourth Museum, for her generosity and expertise; to Evelyn and the staff at Plumas County Museum, for their invaluable assistance; to Maureen Boyd Biro, Gennifer Choldenko, Lynn Hazen, Anne Isaacs, Kathleen Keeler, Sue Corbett, Margaret Dubois, Jane Freeman, Jeanne Miller, Connie Sutton, and Glenys Thomson, for their wisdom; to Marcia Marshall, for bringing the book together; and to my first readers, Art, Lina, and Allison Swislocki, for everything.

A word about images: Some of the illustrations in this book are reprints of those that appeared in James P. Beckwourth's and T. D. Bonner's 1856 biography of the mountain man, *The Life and Adventures of James P. Beckwourth: Mountaineer, Scout, and Pioneer, and Chief of the Crow Nation of Indians,* as well as from period magazines that printed stories about Beckwourth. The integrity of these images has been preserved. See pages 37, 40, 43, 45, 49, 78, and 86.

Twenty-First Century Books
A division of Lerner Publishing Group
241 First Avenue North
Minneapolis, MN 55401 U.S.A.

Website address: www.lernerbooks.com

Library of Congress Cataloging-in-Publication Data

Manheimer, Ann S.
    James Beckwourth: legendary mountain man/by Ann S. Manheimer.
       p.   cm. — (Trailblazer biographies)
    Includes bibliographical references and index.
    ISBN-13: 978–1–57505–892–4 (lib. bdg. : alk. paper)
    ISBN-10: 1–57505–892–8 (lib. bdg. : alk. paper)
    1. Beckwourth, James Pierson, 1798–1866—Juvenile literature.
  2. African American pioneers—West (U.S.)—Biography—Juvenile literature.
  3. African American trappers—West (U.S.)—Biography—Juvenile literature.
  4. Pioneers—West (U.S.)—Biography—Juvenile literature. 5. Trappers—
  West (U.S.)—Biography—Juvenile literature. 6. Frontier and pioneer life—
  West (U.S.)—Juvenile literature. 7. West (U.S.)—Biography—Juvenile
  literature. I. Title. II. Trailblazer biography
    F592.B393M36 2006
    978'.02'092—dc22   2005008477

Manufactured in the United States of America
1 2 3 4 5 6 – JR – 11 10 09 08 07 06

CONTENTS

Introduction 6

1. Into the Howling Wilderness 8

2. Trappers and Storytellers 16

3. Green River Rendezvous 28

4. Chief of the Absaroke 36

5. War, Peace, and Smallpox 46

6. Renown in the Swamplands 56

7. Trader, Horse Thief, and Scout 64

8. Here Is Your Kingdom 74

9. A Polished Gentleman 85

10. The Sand Creek Massacre 92

Epilogue 100

Beckwourth's Sierra Nevada Legacy 101

Beckwourth's Sand Creek
Massacre Testimony 102

Source Notes 105

Selected Bibliography 108

Other Resources 109

Index 110

INTRODUCTION

James Pierson Beckwourth (1798–1866) was a mountain man, one of the few brave men who helped open the American wilderness to settlers. During his adventures in the wilderness, he discovered a new mountain pass over the Sierra Nevada into California's Sacramento Valley. People called it Beckwourth Pass.

Beckwourth was unusual even among unusual men. Most mountain men were white. Jim Beckwourth was black. Most black people in America then were slaves. Jim Beckwourth lived free. Most mountain men died young. Jim Beckwourth lived to be an old man. Like most mountain men, Beckwourth fought Native Americans and called them "savages," yet he adopted their ways, became a chief of the Crow Nation and, eventually, a champion of justice for them. Like most mountain men, Jim Beckwourth could barely read or write, yet he left an autobiography rich with details about the era, the people, and his own remarkable life.

When Beckwourth's book was published, many people did not believe it. They called Jim "a gaudy liar." They said he was "a ruffian of the worst stamp; bloody and treacherous, without honor or honesty." A tale circulated about miners in California who knew

Jim well. They sent a messenger to buy a copy of his book, but the man bought a copy of the Bible by mistake. That evening, reading aloud to the others, he opened the book to the story of Samson and the foxes, in which Samson caught three hundred foxes, tied them together, and set them on fire to burn down the Philistines' cornfields. When the messenger finished reading the tale, one of the listeners cried out, "That'll do! I'd know that story for one of Jim Beckwourth's lies anywhere!"

Still, many who knew Beckwourth—people like the famous mountain men Kit Carson and Jim Bridger—considered him "the most honest trader in the business." And historians, even those who criticized him, have relied on his autobiography in their own writings.

Beckwourth probably exaggerated many details. He lived among people who loved a good tale, and he knew how to tell one. If the numbers and dates in his story aren't always accurate, the heart of it—the dangers he faced, how he survived, and what he learned—tells the truth about the lives of those who survived what he called "the howling wilderness."

As a free black man, Beckwourth never felt fully part of the cultures around him—of what he called the "white" or "civilized" world, of the African American slave culture, or of even the Crow Nation that adopted him.

He never chose any one label. He accepted them all, calling himself, as the title of his autobiography says: "James P. Beckwourth—Mountaineer, Scout, and Pioneer, and Chief of the Crow Nation of Indians."

CHAPTER ONE

INTO THE
HOWLING WILDERNESS

SAINT LOUIS

Nine-year-old James Pierson Beckwourth was riding tall on his horse, partly because he felt so proud and partly because he was sitting on a sack of corn. His father had asked him to take the corn to the mill, two miles away. James was thrilled to be considered man enough for such a job. He was thrilled about riding a horse. He was pleased about going into town. And he was excited at the prospect of visiting friends who lived along the way.

His father had placed the sack of corn on top of a gentle horse and perched Young Jim, as they called him, on top of the sack. While he rode, Jim thought about the happy times he'd spent playing with his friends, all members of the same large neighbor family—eight children in all, ranging in age from one to fourteen.

Spying the fence that separated his friends' house from the road, Jim joyfully rode up to it, only to discover a horrifying scene. All eight children and their parents lay in their yard and doorway, dead. Somehow Jim found enough courage to check their bodies. They were still warm. The killers couldn't be far off.

He raced home, losing the sack of corn along the way, and told his father what had happened. The adults gathered a search party to find the Native Americans who they believed committed the murders. Two days later, the group returned carrying eighteen Native American scalps. It was young Jim's first encounter with the brutality of the wars between the white settlers and Native Americans during the 1800s.

As American settlers moved west onto Native American lands, clashes between the cultures became more frequent and violent. A young James Beckwourth witnessed this violence firsthand.

Jim was born April 26, 1798, in Virginia, the third of thirteen children. His father's last name was Beckwith, but as an adult, Jim used the spelling Beckwourth and made that name famous. Jim had six brothers and six sisters. His father, Jennings Beckwith, was a white plantation owner. He was a soldier during the American Revolution (1775–1783) and, according to some, an officer. Jim's mother was a black slave. Very little is known about her.

When he was quite young, Jim loved hearing battle stories from his father's friends, soldiers from the American Revolution. They would gather at the house, drink peach brandy, and tell their tales. Many years later, Jim remembered how "every eye would dim, and tears [would] course down the cheeks of the old veterans, as they . . . recalled their sufferings during the struggles they had passed through."

In 1805, when Jim was not yet eight years old, the Beckwiths joined one of the earliest waves of white settlers moving west. As Jim described it, Jennings took "all his family and twenty-two Negroes." Although Jim was half black and probably a slave before the family left Virginia, he never referred to himself as anything other than a family member. His father treated him like a son, not a slave, and gave Jim his freedom.

No one knows why Jennings moved his family away from the comforts of the East. It might have been to avoid the racist laws that would not allow a white man to openly marry the black woman he loved. Whatever the reason, Jennings took his family to a land he'd bought outside of Saint Louis, between the forks of the Missouri and Mississippi rivers—"a howling wilderness,'" Jim called it, "inhabited only by wild beasts and merciless savages." The land became known as Beckwith's Settlement.

Hardship and danger were ever present at the settlement. Farming demanded strength and perseverance to clear the endless brush and plow the fertile soil. Children like Jim worked alongside the adults, developing calluses and muscles. Even while they worked, the settlers could never forget the constant threats from their deadly enemies—disease-carrying mosquitoes, wolves and bears, poisonous snakes and, most particularly, Native Americans fighting to save their way of life.

The men in Beckwith's Settlement divided themselves into two groups: one to do the farming and the other to stand armed guard. Neighbors banded together and built blockhouses—log buildings with narrow openings to fire guns through—for refuge during alarms. Alarms rang out almost every day.

Life changed for Jim when, at the age of twelve, he went off to school in Saint Louis. It was a small town then, home to mostly French and Spanish settlers. They traded alcohol, beads, blankets, arms, and ammunition to Native Americans in exchange for furs. In those days, many children, particularly black children, did not attend school. Jim must not have gone to school for very long, because he was unable to write his name until late in his life.

Jim worked as a blacksmith's apprentice in his youth. With more settlers moving West, demand for blacksmiths was high. But Jim wanted more adventurous work.

He apprenticed to (studied under) a Saint Louis blacksmith, George Casner. Jim didn't want the job at first, but he grew to enjoy it, perhaps because blacksmiths were so much in demand. With more settlers moving west, wagons and boats needed building and fixing; horses and mules needed shoeing.

Still, Jim never settled completely into a blacksmith's life. At nineteen he began seeing a young slave named Amy. He stayed out late with her, and then, exhausted and restless, he let his work deteriorate.

One morning blacksmith Casner became so angry at Jim that he threatened to fire him. Equally angry, Jim said he wanted to be fired. Casner, as hot-tempered as Jim, hurled a hammer at him. Jim dodged it and threw it back. They fought. Jim won. Casner fired him. They fought again. Jim won again and decided it was time to leave. But before he could finish packing, a one-armed law officer appeared at the foot of the stairs, demanding to see Jim. Undoubtedly fearing for his safety, Jim waved a loaded pistol and threatened to shoot if the officer came up the steps. The officer left. Certain he'd return any moment with help, Jim made a fast escape.

Jim hid for three days in a friend's house, then shipped out on a shallow, freight-carrying keelboat heading for mines along the Fever River in Illinois. But Casner found him. Perhaps thinking Jennings was Jim's owner, the blacksmith brought Jim to his father—fortunately for Jim.

Father and son confronted each other. Jennings thought Jim ought to make peace with Casner and go back to work. Jim refused. He could never reconcile with that man. Next, Jennings suggested Jim open his own shop in the settlement. But Jim had other ideas. He wanted travel and adventure.

Jennings would not force his son to stay. He must have understood that call to adventure, having answered it himself when he brought his family West. Now it was Jim's turn. Along with plenty of fatherly advice, Jennings gave his son five hundred dollars in cash, a good horse, saddle, and bridle, and wished Jim God speed.

Jim shipped out again, this time with an expedition of eight boats and one hundred men. They were going to ask the Sac and Fox tribes to allow the operation of lead mines near Galena, Illinois. Jim was the hunter for the people on his boat.

Jim found the twenty-day trip upriver slow and tedious. Landing was the exciting part. Both tribes, fully armed, were waiting for them. So, too, were large numbers of U.S. troops stationed in the area. Even though everyone behaved peaceably, Jim was unnerved by the presence of so many Native Americans.

He wasn't the only one. The miners did not trust the Native Americans any more than Native Americans trusted the miners. Throughout the nine days it took to agree on a treaty, every man there stayed armed and alert. Fights broke out regularly.

That all changed when the treaty was signed. Suddenly, gifts appeared—whiskey, guns, knives, blankets. Celebrations began—eating, drinking, singing, dancing, storytelling, wrestling, racing, target shooting. Jim enjoyed himself as much as anyone, and in what must have been quite a surprise, he found himself growing friendly with many Native Americans. He was pleased when they joined his hunting trips and grateful when they showed him their best hunting grounds, abundant with deer, bear, wild turkey, and raccoons. Jim had seen how cruel Native Americans could be. Now he saw another side.

Jim stayed for a year and a half, working in the mines and hunting, until he saved seven hundred dollars. Feeling wealthy, he booked passage on a steamboat down the swirling Mississippi River to New Orleans, famous for both its elegant and rowdy ways. While there, he caught yellow fever. Yellow fever is a serious disease spread by mosquito bites. Its victims become very sick with high fevers, headaches, and backaches.

Two men lie sick and dying from yellow fever in a park in New Orleans, Louisiana, during the 1800s. Jim caught the fever while staying in the city during the early part of that century, but he survived it.

They vomit blood, and their eyes and skin turn yellow from jaundice. Jim was lucky to survive. He went home and stayed with his father while he recuperated.

But he didn't stay long. Jim recovered from the yellow fever, but he'd caught another fever that would plague him the rest of his life—the urge for adventure.

Chapter Two

Trappers
and Storytellers

The Rocky Mountains

"FOR THE ROCKY MOUNTAINS" screamed the bold headline of the ad in the Saint Louis newspapers. The ad continued, looking for "One Hundred Men, to ascend the Missouri to the Rocky Mountains, There to be employed as Hunters." Each man would earn two hundred dollars per year. Anyone interested should apply to General William Ashley.

This was Jim's chance for adventure and money. It was also a good way to escape slave hunters. Although Jennings had gone to court three separate times to declare Jim a free man, slavery was a threat as long as it was legal.

Jim signed up. By the fall of 1824, he had become one of "Ashley's men," employees of the Rocky Mountain Fur Company. General Ashley, a well-known officer and politician, was trying to earn his fortune in the fur business. He led expeditions into the

A trapper in the 1800s. The frontiersman is wearing clothing and carrying gear common to many mountain men and trappers of the time. While not all had horses, most relied on some kind of pack animal, including donkeys and mules.

mountains to trap beavers and other animals, then sold the furs to clothing manufacturers. Beaver fur hats were so popular in those days that beaver pelts, or "plews," as the mountain men called them, were said to be worth more than gold.

Twenty-five men started off in the fall with horses and pack mules. They didn't take much food or clothing. Frontiersmen lived off the land, carrying only what they could not get in the mountains—sugar, flour, coffee, maybe some tea and salt. They wore buckskin and carried an extra pair of leggings. A horn bottle of beaver bait hung from their belts. Bed was a buffalo robe or a blanket roll. Each man needed several knives and a "possibles" sack, hung by a leather thong around the neck. It held tools such as flint and steel for making fire, a bullet mold, and a needle and thread. Their rifles had to be powerful enough to take down a buffalo, a grizzly, or a human attacker. Most of the men carried a pipe and tobacco, and the few who could read sometimes took a Bible or a book of Shakespeare for evenings around the campfire. Each man also carried a fifty-pound leather bag filled with six or more steel traps, folded with their chains wrapped around them.

Jim and his party traveled up the Kansas River from Saint Louis. At night they looked for campsites near water and firewood, with grass for the horses. Unless they were near hostile Native Americans, they built up their campfire after dinner, breathed in the sweet air,

Trappers and Native Americans share stories around a campfire. Beckwourth was a fantastic storyteller, mixing truth and a good deal of invention to entertain his listeners.

gazed at the star-filled sky, and listened to the night sounds—the chomping of horses and mules, the calls of owls, and the howls of coyotes, wolves, and panthers. Then, in the flickering firelight, they told tall tales about great feats of hunting, trapping, fighting, trailing, starving, and feasting. Jim listened carefully and learned the arts of survival and storytelling.

One of the stories Jim told later was about Moses Harris, also called Black Harris because, like Jim, he was African American. One time when the weather turned harsh and food was scarce, Harris offered to travel three hundred miles to the Pawnee village to buy supplies. Known for his strength and endurance, Harris had a reputation for abandoning companions who couldn't keep up with him. When nobody in camp volunteered to go with Harris, Ashley asked Jim to go.

Jim hesitated. Proud as he felt at being chosen for a dangerous and important mission, he didn't want to be abandoned either. He agreed to go only when Harris suggested that Jim lead the way. That way, Harris said, it would be Jim's own fault if he tired out.

The next morning, the two men shouldered their provisions—twenty-five pounds of food each, plus a blanket, rifle, and ammunition—and began their long march. As Jim told the story, he led the way through thirty miles of cold wilderness, stopping only when Harris began to complain. Harris collapsed with exhaustion while Jim built up the fire. They shot wild turkeys that night, enough food for that night and the next day.

After that, however, there weren't any more turkeys or any other game animals. By the time they found the Pawnee village ten days later, they'd run out of food. Both men were hungry, exhausted, and thrilled to reach their goal.

But the camp was deserted. The Native Americans had moved to winter quarters, leaving nothing behind. With no game near the village, Harris and Jim headed toward the Grand Ne-ma-haw River, a branch of the Missouri, searching for food. They marched for two weeks with little more than coffee and sugar to eat. They grew so weak, they had to leave behind their blankets to lighten their load.

Finally, they came across a fresh trail made by Native Americans bringing pelts to a trading post thirty miles away. Jim believed he could make it to the post that night if he traveled alone. But Harris, according to Jim, threw himself to the ground crying, "Oh, Jim, don't leave me; don't leave me here to die! For God's sake stay with me!"

Jim knew they'd both die if he didn't get help, so he set off despite Harris's pleas. He quickly came upon two Osage tribesmen. They took the mountain men to their camp, set out platters of venison, bear meat, and turkey, and invited them to eat. "It is unnecessary to say that I partook of such a meal as I never remember to have eaten before," Jim wrote.

Jim's brush with starvation made him long for civilization. He booked passage home as soon as the ice melted on the Mississippi River and looked forward to spending plenty of time with his father.

But the mountains had changed Jim Beckwourth. Saint Louis was no longer his true home. He ran into General Ashley the day he arrived in town and agreed to go right back to the mountains. After a "flying" visit with friends and family, he set out the next morning with a good horse and instructions to catch up to a party that had already left.

By this time spring was unfolding in the Rockies, spreading greenery and flowers everywhere. The sun glinted off creeks tumbling beneath snow-laden trees. Bird songs echoed off soaring rock walls and called across hidden meadows.

Along with beauty, spring brought the trapping season. Beckwourth learned the mountain man's way to trap. Working with one or two others, he learned to read signs of beavers—piles of twigs and weeds, tooth marks on bark, and mud slides along willow-fringed streams—so he could place his trap near the underwater entrance to the beavers' lodges. With as much secrecy as possible (trappers didn't want rivals to find their beavers), he learned to hide his human scent by wading into the ice-cold water at some distance from the chosen place. At the trapping spot, he had to prepare a level bed about four inches below the surface, lay the trap on it, then stand on the springs to spread the trap's jaws. The next step was to pull the trap's chain to full length into deep water and fasten it to the river bottom with a wooden pole. Trappers also tied the pole to the chain ring so that, if the beaver managed to pull it up, the pole would act as a float to help them find the trap in the morning.

Empty handed after checking his beaver traps, a frontiersman stops to water his horses on his way back to camp. While trapping required a lot of skill, it also involved a good deal of luck.

Then he set the bait by spreading castoreum, a strong-smelling ointment made from beaver glands, on a switch of willow he pushed into the riverbank so that it hung directly over the trap. As he left, he covered his trail with water, leaves, and twigs.

The hunters raised the traps before dawn. Sometimes a beaver might escape by gnawing off his trapped paw, but more often the trapper hauled up a drowned beaver weighing as much as sixty pounds. Beckwourth learned to skin his catch right away in the dim light, then move on to his next trap. When he'd raised all of them—usually six—he would take the skins back to camp for curing, along with the glands.

He'd take the tail too. Although trappers normally ate beaver meat only if nothing else was available, the tail, charred and roasted, was considered a real treat.

Every instant he worked, Beckwourth had to be alert to the country around him. Mountain men traveled without roads, their minds creating maps as they went. Danger was constant. Drowning, infection, snakebites, falls, bears, and human enemies—all could be fatal. Such illnesses as smallpox, tetanus, dysentery, and rabies killed many. Those who survived had to battle rheumatism—pain in the joints—from long hours spent wading in icy streams. At night it was common to see mountain men seated by the fire, rubbing their legs with ointment.

That fall Beckwourth joined Ashley and about seven others in searching for the group Beckwourth had left the previous year. They found them after several days of traveling. Harris was with them and all were well, but their store of food was dangerously low. Like most mountain men, they did not stock up for winter. They ate when there was food and starved when there wasn't.

Game was scarce, and to make matters worse, a three-day snowstorm set in. Without meat, the men were put on a ration of only one cup of flour a day, which they made into a kind of gruel, or thin cereal. Anyone lucky enough to kill a duck or a goose shared it equally with the others.

Flour and an occasional bird were not enough. "No jokes, no fire-side stories, no fun;" Jim recalled, "each man rose in the morning with the gloom of the preceding night filling his mind; we built our fires and partook of our scanty repast without saying a word." They needed large game to survive.

Jim started out from camp alone one morning, weak with hunger. About three hundred yards away, he saw two teal ducks. He leveled his rifle, aimed, shot, and hit his target. He knew he ought to bring the duck back to share with his comrades. That was the custom. That's what his companions would want him to do. But a shared duck would make only a tiny meal, while the entire bird could give Jim strength to hunt for something bigger. His appetite battled his conscience and won. Without ceremony, he built a fire, roasted the duck, and devoured it.

Now he could go on. Within a mile, he killed a large buck. Then he shot a white wolf and three elk. Altogether, they made what Jim called "a pretty good display of meat." He returned near enough to camp to signal his need for help. Cheers rang out when the men saw so much good food.

Still Beckwourth could not keep his thoughts off the teal duck. Even though his friends agreed he'd done the right thing, Jim knew that if he hadn't found any game, guilt would have haunted him the rest of his life. From then on, he vowed, he would always share his food, money, or blankets with friends.

Beckwourth's luck in hunting held the next day when he shot what he thought was an enormous bear. It turned out to be his first bison kill, although people then called such animals buffalo. No animal meant more to mountain men's survival. They loved its rich, tender meat—boiled, fried, or roasted—for any or all meals of the day. Native Americans mixed its pulverized meat with dried berries to make pemmican, a high-energy food that didn't spoil. Bison herds helped Beckwourth's group travel during winter storms by beating down snowdrifts. This created paths and exposed grass for the horses.

That harsh winter, Ashley's men roamed the southern fork of the Platte River into lands only Native Americans had seen before. The men had to sleep on frozen ground with only twigs and maybe a blanket for bedding. When game was scarce, they ate whatever they had. When all else was gone, mountain men sometimes even ate their own moccasins. When horses died along the trail or were stolen by Native Americans, Beckwourth and his companions had to shoulder the one-hundred-pound packs themselves.

Snow fell well into April, making passage so difficult that the men left the bank of a small stream they'd been following and cut west across the country. To their amazement, on April 19, 1825, they came upon a large and beautiful river, later called the Green River, surrounded by acres of land covered with bison. They stayed for several days, resting and hunting. Along with the bison and geese, they found teals. Beckwourth stayed away from the ducks.

Ashley split his group into four smaller parties for spring trapping. Beckwourth's group went north along Horse Creek, where beaver were so plentiful that the men moved slowly, sometimes staying extra nights at a campsite. In just a few days, they brought in more than one hundred beaver skins, worth about sixteen hundred dollars in Saint Louis—quite a lot of money then. It was a good, easy time, with gentle weather and plenty of game. Along the way, Beckwourth became close friends with seventeen-year-old Baptiste La Jeunesse. Beckwourth had helped the boy several times, and Baptiste had come to think of Beckwourth as a father.

But gentle times never lasted long in the mountains. A group of sixteen Native Americans joined them as they camped along the beaver-laden creek. The trappers could not identify their tribe, but the men claimed to be friendly, and at first, they acted that way. Beckwourth grew suspicious when he saw them poking into the trappers' belongings and handling their guns. When other hunters also grew uncomfortable, they moved camp toward open country where they could defend themselves better against an attack.

The attack came before they reached the prairie. One night, when everyone was asleep except a guard named Le Brache, a yell for help and the crack of a gunshot rang out. A bullet passed between Beckwourth and Baptiste, burning a hole in Beckwourth's blankets. It was Jim's first hostile encounter with Native Americans as a mountain man, and he was scared. "We were all up in an instant. An Indian had seized my rifle, but I instantly wrenched it from him, though, I acknowledge, I was too terrified to shoot." After the struggle, Beckwourth found Le Brache dead from a tomahawk wound. The Native Americans had disappeared from the camp and were hiding

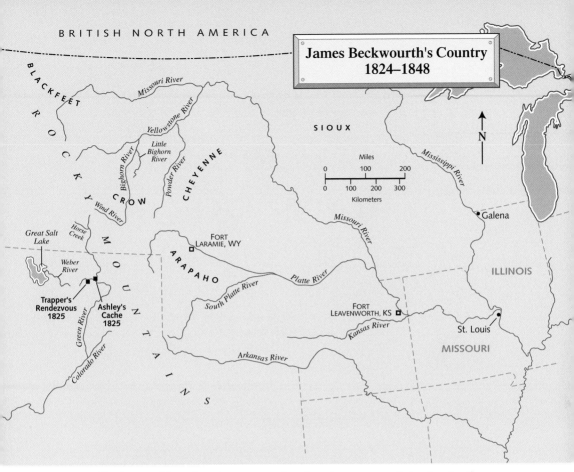

Beckwourth's adventures as a hunter, trapper, and trader in the Rocky Mountains took him throughout the midwestern and western United States during the years 1824 to 1848.

in the surrounding bushes. The trappers packed hastily, then raced for open ground through a gauntlet of bullets and arrows fired by the Native Americans. No one else was hurt, although two horses were wounded.

A couple of days later, Beckwourth returned with Baptiste and a few others. Their comrade's body was gone, but they named the nearby creek Le Brache, after him. Then they checked the traps they'd set out before the attack. They found a beaver in almost every one.

CHAPTER THREE
GREEN RIVER RENDEZVOUS

THE ROCKY MOUNTAINS

That July, Beckwourth returned to the Green River for a rendezvous, or gathering, of Ashley's mountain men. In the months leading up to the rendezvous, Ashley had provisions brought in from Saint Louis and buried, or cached, at agreed locations along the river. He also posted signs directing his men to the place to meet on July 1, 1825. The trappers came to be paid for their pelts and to buy supplies for the next season.

Since no trapping was done in midsummer, mountain men could stay at the rendezvous for weeks. Hundreds came, and so did Native American men, women, and children. The meeting started as business but quickly turned into a wild carnival, with gambling, racing, drinking, flirting, bragging, wrestling, shooting, and general rowdiness. The money the trappers took in immediately went out again, as much for whiskey and women as for provisions. General Ashley

A bend of the Green River—which runs through what would become Wyoming and Utah—as it appeared during Beckwourth's lifetime. Ashley cached provisions along the river in preparation for the 1825 rendezvous with his mountain men.

made a good profit too—especially on sales of whiskey, which he could buy in Saint Louis for thirty cents a gallon and resell in the mountains for more than twenty dollars.

By the end of the rendezvous in 1825, Ashley had a fortune in pelts. The next task was to get them to Saint Louis without losing any along the way. Ashley selected a group of twenty men, including Beckwourth, to return to civilization with the furs. On the trip back, they endured two attacks by Native Americans—Beckwourth was wounded in one battle—and one by a grizzly bear.

They arrived in Saint Louis on September 19. A huge crowd greeted them at the marketplace. Jennings was there, overjoyed to see his son. Jim, however, was saddened to see how much his father had aged.

That didn't keep Jim from celebrating his return. He and his friends drank and partied at a local hotel for two days. General Ashley paid for it all with his new-found fortune.

Beckwourth stayed in Saint Louis for a week before agreeing to return to the mountains. This time, he went reluctantly, perhaps because of Eliza, the new sweetheart he had to leave behind. He also said farewell to his father.

Jim spent that winter at the Great Salt Lake near the mouth of the Weber River. Winter quarters were similar in many ways to the summer rendezvous. Since it was between trapping seasons, other than tending to survival needs, the men could relax. Hundreds of people came from all around—mountaineers, their wives, Native American families—and created a small village. That winter they were also joined by thousands of members of the Snake tribe. Beckwourth's group had unknowingly camped on the Snakes' regular winter grounds. The Snakes didn't seem to mind. They built hundreds of lodges in the village and invited the frontiersmen to visit their lodges and attend their religious ceremonies. Beckwourth was fascinated. He took every opportunity to watch and learn Native American ways.

At the rendezvous the next summer, 1826, Ashley announced that he was selling his Rocky Mountain Fur Company to frontiersmen William L. Sublette, Jedediah Smith, and David E. Jackson. Before he left, the general told Beckwourth he admired his courage but worried about his recklessness. "It is my hearty

Frontiersmen and Native Americans gather for a rendezvous during the 1800s. Begun by Ashley in 1825, the gatherings became a tradition among the usually solitary mountain men, giving them a chance to trade goods and take part in rowdy games. Beckwourth enjoyed the annual meetings.

desire to have you do well, and live to a good old age," the general said and advised Beckwourth to stop risking his life just to prove his bravery.

But Jim Beckwourth found risks impossible to avoid, particularly in land inhabited by Blackfeet, who were at war with whites. He had many battles with them. The most famous occurred when he was guiding a group of about fifty men, women, and children to the 1828 rendezvous. Hundreds of Blackfeet chased them for six miles, into a patch of willows. With a lake on one side and mountains on the other, the grove of trees provided good cover. Approaching Blackfeet would be shot. But ammunition was low, and the mountaineers could not hold out for long.

The men needed help. They knew that other mountain men were nearby, also heading toward the rendezvous. All they needed was someone to bolt heroically through the Blackfoot lines, survive the attack, outrace pursuers, and get aid. It was Jim Beckwourth's kind of job. "Give me a swift horse," he said, "and I will try to force my way."

Jim and Calhoun, set off in Native American clothing. "The balls and arrows flew around us like hail," Jim recalled, "but we escaped uninjured."

They sped along for five miles before finding friends. Soon they were rushing back to the willows, the road behind them filled with mountain men racing to the rescue. Beckwourth and Calhoun again rode through the Blackfoot lines, to a chorus of cheers from their friends. The Blackfeet, surprised at the line of men riding into the battle, gave up the fight. "[N]ever in my whole life had I run such danger of losing my life and scalp," Beckwourth said. "I now began to deem myself Indian-proof, and to think I never should be killed by them."

At the rendezvous, Jim learned that the Blackfeet were making peace with a neighboring tribe, the Salishes, or Flatheads. He welcomed peace because, he said, war was bad for trade. Perhaps still thinking of himself as "Indian-proof," he offered to help start a trading post in Blackfoot country, even though the tribe knew he had killed many of their warriors. He said Native Americans respected courage and battle-field skills, even in their enemies. Beckwourth lived peaceably among the Blackfeet for nearly a month.

The friendly relationship ended when a large group of Blackfeet spied Jim on foot one day, searching with a friend for lost horses. Also on foot, the Blackfeet—for no reason that Beckwourth could identify—started to chase the two mountain men. Telling his friend to hide by the creek, Beckwourth took off. He raced across the stream and lost sight of the Blackfeet until he reached the summit of a small hill. The Native Americans saw him too and, with a yell, kept up the chase. "On, on we tore;" Beckwourth said. "I to save my scalp, and my pursuers to win it."

He headed straight for the main camp of trappers, but it was empty. The men had left for the river, forty-five miles away. Jim's "Indian-proof" feeling vanished that instant. "The Indians were close at my heels; the bullets were whizzing past me; their yells sounded painfully in my ears; and I could almost feel the knife making a circuit round my skull."

He bounded on, following the road left by his friends. Scorched with thirst, mile after mile he raced ahead of their bullets, ignoring hunger and exhaustion. Finally, he said, "the glorious sight of camp-smoke" came into view. His friends recognized him from a mile away and rode out to meet him. Then it was the Blackfeet's turn to be chased. The mountain men pursued them to the river, where most of the Native Americans escaped under the cover of night.

Beckwourth's legs were so swollen from the run that he had trouble walking for several days. With a storyteller's math, he estimated that he'd run a ninety-five-mile race for his life.

That September a group of friendly Crows visited the trappers and asked to meet the men who fought Blackfeet so well. The trappers pointed out Beckwourth. Caleb Greenwood, a mountain man who spoke the Crow language fluently, answered many questions about Jim. But he soon grew tired of telling the truth. Instead, he said that Jim was a Crow who had been captured when he was a child. Many Crow women had lost children and wondered if Jim might be their son. All the while, Jim said nothing, enjoying the joke.

Later, when the mountain men split into smaller groups to trap, Jim went with the group going into Crow country. He welcomed the relief of traveling among friendly tribes, "to be in a place where we could rest from our unsleeping vigilance, and to feel, when we rose in the morning, there was some probability of our living till night." Saying good-bye to his friend Baptiste and to the other frontiersmen, Beckwourth turned his journey toward Absaroke, the Crow name for both the tribe and the land where they lived.

Checking his traps early one morning along the Powder River, Beckwourth found that one was missing. The trap, the float pole, and any beaver that might have been caught were nowhere to be found. The next morning, he and his companion, the famous mountain man Jim Bridger, spied a creature at some distance. They rushed at it and found Beckwourth's lost trap, with beaver and float pole attached. Apparently, the chain had tangled around a bison, which dragged it out of the river and onto land. Jim was glad

Beckwourth finds his trapped beaver downstream along the Powder River. That night the "stolen" beaver provided quite a story.

to have not only the pelt and the solution to the mystery but also another story to tell. That evening at camp, he dramatically announced that the missing trap had been stolen.

"Stolen!" The others exclaimed.

"Yes, it was stolen by a buffalo [bison]."

Jim was thoroughly enjoying his tall tale. But one of his listeners did not see the humor. He accused Beckwourth of lying and threw a punch at him. The two men fought and went for their guns. Others came between them, and advised Beckwourth to leave camp for a few days to cool down. That night he left on a trapping trip with Jim Bridger.

He never went back.

CHAPTER FOUR

CHIEF OF
THE ABSAROKE

THE ROCKY MOUNTAINS

Beckwourth and Bridger followed a small stream until it forked. There, they separated, promising to find each other again after they set their traps. Beckwourth traveled up his side of the stream searching for beaver. Instead, he found himself surrounded by Native Americans. With no way to defend himself, he gave them his gun and all his possessions. As they marched him to their camp, he desperately hoped they'd show him mercy.

From a far hill, Jim Bridger watched the men he thought were Cheyennes take Beckwourth away. He was certain his friend was as good as dead and said as much back at camp. That night the mountain men mourned for Beckwourth by telling stories of his daring exploits.

Meanwhile, Jim was being welcomed by Crows, who thought he was their long-lost relative. One of the

36

men, Big Bowl, announced that Jim was his son who had been kidnapped years before. Jim's new sisters dressed him in fancy clothing. His new brothers gave him twenty fine horses. He was given a new name, Morning Star, and a new wife, Still Waters. He was welcomed with the kind of affection and respect he never received from white people. He decided to stay.

Money was another reason to stay. Even though he no longer worked for the Rocky Mountain Fur Company, he owed his former employer $275 for goods he'd bought from the company. He had promised to pay his debt with beaver furs and was looking forward

This illustration from an old book about Beckwourth shows members of the Crow Nation during the 1800s. Beckwourth was welcomed by the Crows, who thought he was one of their own.

to hunting for those furs on Crow land. As a member of the Absarokes, he would have complete freedom to do just that. Jim wanted more than freedom to hunt, however. He also wanted the tribe's help with trapping and trading. To get that, he needed status in the tribe. He decided to become a chief.

Crow chiefs did not necessarily govern. The title was earned by making "coups," or brave deeds, during war. To become a chief, a Crow had to lead a successful raid, capture a horse tied in an enemy's camp, snatch an enemy's gun or bow, and be the first to touch an enemy, whether or not the enemy was wounded. Lightly tapping an enemy with a coup stick earned higher honors than killing him.

War was a major part of Absaroke life and religion, but skill and courage were valued more than killing. All war acts were supposed to be inspired by religious visions. Religious ceremonies included prayers and stories about battles. The entire tribe was involved, women as well as men. Warriors were given new names to celebrate brave deeds. The most honored leaders were those who lost no warriors in battle.

Jim, however, had learned to fight to kill, and his method succeeded. In those days, Crows constantly fought with other tribes for horses or for revenge. Beckwourth's deadly approach brought both.

It took Jim less than two weeks to earn coups. He was the first to kill one of the enemy during a raid. He took not only the enemy's gun, but also his lance, war club, bow, and quiver (case) of arrows. The warriors celebrated Beckwourth's achievement by painting their faces black with a mixture of charcoal and blood, riding through the Crow village singing and shouting, and giving gifts to their families and friends. Beckwourth earned a new name— Antelope.

It didn't take long for him to feel at home. He quickly learned to speak Crow fluently. He let his hair grow, wore only Crow clothing, and with dark skin, he looked and sounded like one of them. It was no surprise that on his first trip to a trading post with his Native American companions, none of the white traders wondered about him. When the Crows were nearly finished with their business, one of them asked the clerk for "be-has-i-pe-hish-a." The clerk did not understand. Jim watched the confusion in amusement for a few moments, then spoke up. "Gentlemen," he said in his perfect English, "that Indian wants scarlet cloth."

He thoroughly enjoyed the surprise that followed. "If a bomb-shell had exploded in the fort they could not have been more astonished," he said. The clerks quizzed him about who he was and where he'd grown up. Finally, they asked his name. "Good heavens!" they exclaimed. "You were supposed dead."

Beckwourth became a well-respected chief, with several lodges and wives. Absaroke marriage was quite different from marriage among white people— men could marry many women, and women could leave marriages easily or be with more than one man.

Jim had at least eight wives when he fell in love with the one woman who refused to marry him.

Pine Leaf **(above)** was a strong woman warrior. She vowed to kill one hundred enemy warriors to avenge her brother's death.

Pine Leaf—Bar-chee-am-pe in Crow—had lost her twin brother during an attack on the village when she was twelve years old. She vowed that she would never marry until she had avenged his death by killing one hundred of the enemy. The men laughed when she joined war parties, but she quickly proved herself in battle. She was already an accomplished warrior when she caught Jim's attention.

Charmed by her spirit and intelligence as well as her looks, Beckwourth described her as "one of the bravest women that ever lived . . . endowed with extraordinary strength, with the activity of the cat and the speed of the antelope." As they rode into battle one day, he asked her to marry him. She said he had too many wives already, but Jim persisted. Finally, laughing, she promised to marry him "when the pine-leaves turn yellow."

It took Jim a couple of days to realize that pine leaves do not turn yellow. He'd been tricked. He gave up asking and instead decided to help her complete her vow in battle.

Beckwourth was torn between war and trade. Battle deeds brought influence with the Crows, and trade brought money. He paid off his debt to the Rocky Mountain Fur Company and accepted a position with its rival, the American Fur Company. His job was to help the company trade with the Crows. His salary, he said, allowed him to dress his wives better than any other women in the tribe.

In the fall of 1833, Thomas Fitzpatrick, who had been one of Ashley's men with Beckwourth and became co-owner of the Rocky Mountain Fur Company, came to the Big Horn River with a party of trappers. While he was away from his camp to visit the Crow village, a group of young Crows stole his provisions, guns, horses, and pelts. Although the Crows later returned some of what they took, the Rocky Mountain Company suffered a huge loss.

Evidence suggested that traders working for Beckwourth's employer, the American Fur Company, were behind the theft. Even though several traders from American Fur were in the area, many people blamed Jim. He strongly denied it. He claimed that he saved the lives of Fitzpatrick's men and rescued the goods. Still, many thought he was guilty.

That didn't change Jim's high standing among the Absarokes. As he put it, his medicine—meaning spiritual power—was "always considered good and true." He was so respected that his military advice was often followed even over that of other chiefs.

On the morning of November 21, 1834, Beckwourth led the Crows into one of the bloodiest recorded battles between Native American tribes. A Crow hunting party had come upon a large group of Blackfeet on Absaroke land. The two tribes had long been enemies. The Crows chased the Blackfeet into a natural stone fort, a huge wall of granite that surrounded the top of the hill.

When Beckwourth heard the war cries, he galloped toward the fight, sending messengers to the nearby village for help. About seven hundred Crows came, including every man, woman, and child able to point a gun or mount a horse. But the Crows could not get through the Blackfeet's walled defense. Several Crows were killed trying. Chief Long Hair (whose hair was said to be eleven feet long) called for the tribe to turn back.

"No, hold!" Beckwourth cried. Speaking from a high rock, he said, "If we attempt to run from here, we shall be shot in the back." He believed they could win by storming the fort. Urging the Crows to join him, Jim leaped from the rock and raced to the fort without glancing behind. The others followed. With some of the best fighters positioned on one side of the fort to attract attention, Jim led a charge over the opposite wall.

Beckwourth and the Crows fight the Blackfeet in November 1834 at the natural fort in what became Colorado. The Crows won the bloody battle.

The battle that followed was not long, but it was horrifying. "The clash of battle-axes, and the yells of the opposing combatants were truly appalling," Jim said. "Many [Blackfeet] leaped the wall only to meet their certain doom below." The rock grew slippery as blood pooled inside the fort, giving off what Jim called a "sickening smell." After the Crows won the fight, they tormented the wounded Blackfeet until all of them were dead. When Blackfeet won battles, they treated their enemies with equal cruelty.

Even though he'd been the one to convince the Crows to attack, Beckwourth was horrified by the cruelty he saw that day. He thought about leaving Absaroke, but he knew brutality was not practiced only by Native Americans. "Some of the very worst savages I ever saw in the Rocky Mountains were white men." he said. He also did not want to abandon his friends and loved ones or lose the opportunity to hunt with the Absarokes.

About forty Crow warriors were killed in the battle. The tribe went into mourning. In a tradition that particularly bothered Jim, grieving Crows bloodied themselves by cutting off parts of their fingers and gashing their foreheads.

In the spring, when chokecherries bloomed, the tribe celebrated a more peaceful ritual. Then the Absarokes gathered to plant tobacco, which was sacred to them. A tribal officer—the mixer—chose the site. In 1834 he selected the Little Bighorn River in what is now Montana. Special ceremonies with songs, drums, pipe smoking, storytelling, and prayers continued for two days. At the end, the tribe held a race to bring the tobacco seeds to the garden. The winner earned coups and expected to have good luck that season.

After the ritual was over in 1834, the head chief, Arapooish (Rotten Belly), one of the greatest Crow chiefs, surprised everyone by announcing that he was stepping down. Then he insisted on going with Beckwourth on a war raid. Jim was concerned that Arapooish had become what the Crows called a "Crazy-Dog-wishing-to-die," someone pledged to do something in battle that would lead to his own death. He tried to convince Arapooish not to fight. The old chief would not be dissuaded.

Announcing he was ready to die, Arapooish charged first in the battle, wheeling his horse and cutting with his ax. He killed two of the enemy before an arrow struck him down. The rest of the Crows quickly won the battle, then gathered around their dying leader. Arapooish's last deeds, Jim said, were to appoint him the next head chief and to give him his shield—a high honor—and a medal that came from William Clark of the Lewis and Clark expedition, the first official exploration of the West. Then the great chief died.

The shrieks and blood of mourning that followed were worse than any Beckwourth had witnessed before. They lasted for two days. Then, according to Beckwourth's accounts, he and his old friend, Long Hair, were pronounced cochiefs in charge of the tribe, although there is now way to verify this. After Arapooish's funeral, Jim was given his final Crow name: Nan-kup-bah-pah, or Medicine Calf. He had reached the height of fame in the Absaroke Nation.

In this illustration from Beckwourth's biography, Chief Arapooish hands his shield to Beckwourth (*standing at right*). The mountain man claimed that the leader's dying act made him a new chief of the Absaroke.

CHAPTER FIVE
WAR, PEACE, AND SMALLPOX

THE ROCKY MOUNTAINS

In his first speech as chief, Beckwourth—called Medicine Calf—told the Crows, "I want all my warriors to lay aside the battle-axe and lance for a season, and turn their attention to hunting and trapping."

Even though he called for peace, Beckwourth didn't know how to create it. He thought he could force peace by turning the Absaroke Nation into such a terrible force that it would make its enemies fear to attack it. Then, he said, they could all "turn their battle-axes into beaver-traps, and their lances into hunting knives."

It didn't work. The cycle of horse raids and war parties continued. One wintry day, Beckwourth set out with fifty warriors to raid a Cheyenne village a few days' ride away. The weather was so cold that, Beckwourth said, the buffalo would come close enough to the fire to be shot without a man stirring from his seat. Beckwourth and his group started to cross a wide plain when a violent storm descended.

"We all became saturated with the driving rain and hail, and our clothing and robes were frozen stiff;" Beckwourth said, "still we kept moving, as we knew it would be certain death to pause on our weary course. The winds swept irresistible violence across the desert prairie, and we could see no shelter to protect us from the freezing blast."

Eventually they took cover from the wind in a large gully where, exhausted, they fell asleep. When Beckwourth woke, so much snow had fallen on him that it took all his strength to get out from underneath it. To stay in the gully, he knew, meant death. Painfully, he forced himself up and soon found a dry creek protected by a cave of snow, with a pile of dead wood nearby. He built a fire and brought the others to the new shelter. Only after they had warmed themselves by the fire did they realize that they'd left two men behind. The two left in the gully died from the cold.

The deaths threw the village into the bloody mourning rituals that Beckwourth hated. The self-mutilation and wailing didn't end until Beckwourth and a couple of friends managed to escape from a Blackfoot attack a while later. Battles like those were so common that sometimes Beckwourth barely made note of them. For example, he described one journey as "without accident, except sustaining [suffering] another siege from the Black Feet."

War was also part of a major Crow ceremony, the Sun Dance. This ceremony took place every three or four years, when someone in mourning wanted a religious vision to help avenge the death of a loved one killed in battle. It spread over several days and involved complex rituals with sacred dolls, music, pipe smoking, special clothing, and war stories.

Part of the ceremony was the selection of a virtuous woman to be the tree-notcher, whose job was to tap a tree representing the enemy. Being chosen was a great honor. The woman had to be absolutely faithful to her husband and would not be allowed to remarry if her husband died. Any man who had evidence against the woman was required to speak out. If anyone did, the woman would be ridiculed or even beaten.

Jim's youngest wife, Nom-ne-dit-chee—whom he called Little Wife—had longed to become a tree-notcher since she was a child. When her turn came, she modeled her fanciest clothes for him. For fine occasions, Crow women usually wore long deerskin dresses decorated with elk teeth and jewelry such as bear-claw necklaces or buffalo bone earrings. They parted their hair in the middle and perfumed it with bear grease, castoreum, and sweet herbs. Jim admired his wife as he applied the ritual paints to her.

Her name was called, and she presented herself at the door of the medicine lodge, saying: "[I]f there be a warrior, or any other man under the sun, who knows anything wrong in me, or injurious to my virtue, let him speak." Next, she carried sand, wood, and elk chips into the medicine lodge, passing through two

Warrior-Chief Beckwourth sits on his horse, shield and spear in hand. As a leader of the Crows, he led warriors on raids and into fierce battles.

lines of warriors who could challenge her selection as tree-notcher.

Beckwourth had no way of knowing if other men could or would speak against her. He worried as he watched, then felt a flood of relief and pride as Nom-ne-dit-chee. walked through without objection. Officers of the ceremony passed their hands over her head, shoulders, and arms, and proclaimed her a virtuous woman.

After the ceremony, Beckwourth returned to his routines of hunting, horse raids, and war parties. One trip took him south with a small group of warriors to Arapaho country to buy, trade, or steal more horses for his tribe. They were gone for so long that most of the tribe thought they'd been killed. He relished the tribe's joyful surprise when he and his companions rode in, driving hundreds of horses in front of them.

In the midst of the rejoicing, Beckwourth's Crow father, Big Bowl, asked if he could raise Black Panther, the son of Beckwourth and Nom-ne-dit-chee. This was not unusual among the Absarokes, and Jim agreed.

When Beckwourth visited the fort with the tribe a short time later, he had fun once again, watching the astonishment of the white traders who, like the Crows, thought he'd been killed. He also enjoyed the welcome the traders gave Black Panther. They showered the boy and his mother with gifts. Beckwourth was less happy with the language they taught his son. He learned to swear in both French and English. But Beckwourth believed Black Panther would forget the words as soon as he returned to the tribe. Crows, he said, did not drink whiskey or use profanity.

Jim had spent more than ten years in the mountains. He had gone from youth to middle age in Absaroke. He began to take stock of his life: "Year after year had rolled away, and now that I had attained middle life, they seemed to pass me with accelerated [faster] pace, and the question would intrude upon my mind, What had I done? . . . I had traversed the . . . far Rocky Mountains in summer heats and winter frosts; I had encountered savage beasts and wild men, until my deliverance was a prevailing miracle. . . . I had . . . dyed my hand crimson with the blood of victims who had never injured me. . . . And what had I to show for so much wasted energy, and such a catalogue of ruthless deeds? . . .

In good truth," he decided, "I found I had simply wasted my time." On July 15, 1836, Beckwourth boarded the boat for Saint Louis, promising to return to the Crows the next green grass.

Saint Louis had changed as much as Beckwourth had. Once a rowdy settlement of muddy streets, it had become a major center of trade and entertainment. New warehouses and taverns lined its waterfront. New buildings fronted its streets, and grand mansions of wealthy businessmen dotted the outskirts.

Jim made his way through the transformed streets to the home of his sister Lou. At first, she didn't recognize the powerfully built man in her doorway, wearing animal skins decorated with intricate beadwork and with long black hair hanging to his hips. Then she yelled out, "My God! It is my brother!" and flew into his arms.

His sister had sad news for him. His beloved father, Jennings, had returned to Virginia a few years earlier and had died there. His brothers were scattered about the country. Many of his friends were dead. Eliza, the sweetheart he'd left behind, had married someone else. Saint Louis was not the secure, happy haven Jim was looking for.

Beckwourth felt lost and spent much of his time wandering aimlessly. He heard rumors of threats against his life stemming from the robbery of Fitzpatrick's camp. One afternoon Fitzpatrick and four rough companions came into a bar where Beckwourth was having a drink. "There's the Crow," Fitzpatrick said, pointing to him. The thugs attacked Jim with knives.

Weaponless, Beckwourth dove behind the counter and hurled glasses at his attackers until a friend handed him a large knife. He left his cover and challenged the others to move first. As he was deciding whether to give the Crow war whoop, the sheriff came forward, urging calm. Threatened with jail, Beckwourth cooperated.

Not long afterward, Beckwourth talked with Fitzpatrick and his partner, William Sublette, about the incident. When Fitzpatrick described the robbery, Sublette said it was absurd to think Beckwourth guilty. Although Jim had a reputation as a rough mountain man, his employers said he was honest. Fitzpatrick apologized, and the two renewed their friendship.

Beckwourth made time to call on another old friend, General Ashley. Jim's self-assurance left him the moment the general's wife answered the door. Intimidated by her beauty as well as by the elegant home, he grew painfully aware that his mountain manners did not fit into Saint Louis high society. He finally relaxed when Ashley arrived, and the two could talk about his time among the Crows.

Perhaps those reminiscences convinced Beckwourth to go back to the Absarokes in the spring of 1837. He made the journey of 2,750 miles with remarkable speed, arriving in just fifty-three days. Shortly after he returned, Bar-chee-am-pe (Pine Leaf) announced that she had completed her vow of killing more than one hundred of the enemy. With Medicine Calf—Beckwourth—back, she said, she would finally marry him and perhaps keep him from leaving again. She placed her hand under Jim's chin and lifted his head. "This day I become your wife," she said. "Bar-chee-am-pe is a warrior no more."

Jim happily shook hands with the braves around him, then told stories of his adventures while Pine Leaf dressed for the short marriage ceremony. When she returned, clothed in a Crow woman's elegance, Jim barely recognized her. He spoke of their wedding with a touch of sadness: "Pine Leaf, the pride and admiration of her people, was no longer the dauntless and victorious warrior, the avenger of the fall of her brother. She retired from the field of her glory, and became the affectionate wife of the Medicine Calf."

Almost immediately after they married, Beckwourth returned to his old routines. He led a hunting expedition and returned to find horses stolen by Blackfeet. Then he led a war party to recover them. He was back in the life he had tried to leave.

The weather was pleasant that spring of 1837, and the traders and Native Americans were looking forward to the arrival of the *St. Peter*, the American Fur Company steamboat that brought goods to the wilderness every year. In 1837, however, the *St. Peter* brought more than goods. It also brought a killer deadlier than any warrior—smallpox.

People on the *St. Peter* were infected with this dreaded disease, which had come from Europe more than one hundred years before. By 1837 the Native Americans of the plains had already suffered two outbreaks of it. Victims came down with pox, aches, fever, vomiting, and delirium. Bodies of victims turned

This illustration shows Native Americans suffering from the "pox" (smallpox). Brought to America from Europe, the disease killed many thousands of Native Americans.

black and swelled to three times their normal size. The illness was so horrible that some people chose to kill themselves instead of suffering the symptoms. Among Native Americans, death was almost certain.

The epidemic of 1837 was the deadliest yet. Hundreds died every day, too many even to bury. Bodies were thrown over cliffs or left where they lay in huts, doorways, or cornfields. The stench spread for miles as the disease ravaged across the prairies, into valleys and mountains, leaving behind empty villages and many thousands dead.

Fortunately for the Crows, they were away on a hunting trip along the Wind River when the disease arrived at their usual trading post. They heard about it and stayed away. They remembered the earlier epidemics too well—one of their shrines, the Place of Skulls, was located where two of their ancestors had jumped off a cliff rather than suffer from the illness.

Perhaps because his tribe suffered less than others, Beckwourth became the target of another false charge, worse than any other ever aimed at him—that he brought the epidemic to the Native Americans. The details varied. One story said he stole infected blankets and sold them to the Blackfeet. Another said he was ill himself and passed on the disease. There was no truth to any of the accusations.

But the epidemic affected Beckwourth, as it did everyone in the region. In addition to the misery it caused, it killed many clients of and suppliers for the fur companies. That, combined with the dwindling numbers of beaver and buffalo, meant the business that had supported Beckwourth for more than fifteen years was declining. In 1838 Beckwourth's employer, the American Fur Company, refused to rehire him.

If he'd been rehired, Jim said, he might have stayed with the Absarokes to the end of his days. As it turned out, perhaps because he lost his job or perhaps because of his weariness with endless horse raids and war parties, Beckwourth decided to leave his tribe. He and Pine Leaf had been married for only five weeks. Saying good-bye was painful. Promising to return in four seasons, he boarded the boat back to Saint Louis.

CHAPTER SIX
RENOWN IN
THE SWAMPLANDS

FLORIDA

Beckwourth was in Saint Louis for barely a week when a general asked if he wanted to go to the Florida Territory to fight Native Americans there. Jim said no. He was tired of war.

The Seminoles—whose name comes from a Spanish word meaning "wild and untamed"—were living on a reservation in southern Florida. Runaway slaves had found refuge with the tribe and married into it. The reservation land was poor, but white settlers wanted to take it away from the Seminoles anyway. This was partly because they feared that the runaway slaves and Seminoles would unite against them. The U.S. government drove the Seminoles off the land, into woods and swamps, forcing them to give up their traditional hunting and agriculture. Instead, they lived off swamp cabbage, bark, fish, and whatever else was available. Many Seminoles fled into the wilderness of

Seminoles attack a U.S. fort to defend their lands in Florida during the Second Seminole War (1835–1842). A U.S. Army general persuaded Beckwourth to join the fight in 1837.

the Florida Everglades, attacking from their hiding places in the tall grass of the swamplands.

Since the U.S. Army needed someone with Beckwourth's kind of skills to fight the Seminoles, the general did not give up trying to persuade Jim. He made a promise Beckwourth could not refuse: renown, a chance to become famous. Jim's old friend William Sublette, who was also there, advised him to accept. Calling Florida "a delightful country," Sublette predicted Beckwourth would enjoy the change.

Finally convinced, Jim agreed. He signed up sixty-four volunteers to work under him as muleteers, taking care of the army's horses and mules. They all boarded a steamer to New Orleans, where on October 26, 1837, they met the *Maid of New York*, the ship that would carry them to Florida's "fields of renown."

The journey across the Gulf of Mexico was Jim's first ocean voyage, and he was miserable with seasickness. His men drove the horses on board, but mountaineers had no experience riding the sea. They stowed the animals in the ship's hold without securing them in place. When they ran into heavy storms, the horses were tossed about. Many were hurt. Others died and had to be thrown overboard.

The journey came to a halt when the ship ran onto a reef. The men were stranded for twelve days, slammed by waves. Water filled the boat's hold. For Beckwourth, accustomed to roaming freely across the wide wilderness, being trapped on a small ship was painful. Renown seemed very far away.

He was nearing the end of his endurance when a passing steamer saw their plight and brought the news to the army in Florida. Rescued and on land again, Beckwourth could finally settle into his new job. He was one of the most highly paid civilian employees of the army, receiving fifty dollars a month as an express rider, a warrant officer, master teamster, muleteer, and assistant wagon master. He worked alongside six hundred other Missourians, called Missouri Volunteers and Morgan's Spies. The volunteers typically earned only eight dollars per month plus forty cents a day for their horses. They were all under the command of a popular colonel, Richard Gentry.

Beckwourth's wilderness skills qualified him for one of the most dangerous jobs in the service, carrying dispatches, or messages, between army outposts.

Shortly after arriving, he was asked to carry messages to General Thomas Jesup, stationed one hundred miles away. The army had already lost nine couriers trying to reach that outpost.

Years of experience had taught Beckwourth to "act the 'wolf'" while traveling through country controlled by Native Americans. He avoided known trails, journeying alone or with only one or two companions. He knew how to read the signs left by others: footprints, bent twigs, far-off sounds.

He set off at sunrise through the junglelike swamp with its watery ground, fallen trees and tangled undergrowth, and poisonous snakes and alligators. Small hummocks, or rounded mounds of grass and soil, ran like islands through the swamps. Since the area was unfamiliar, Beckwourth kept the landmarks in sight as he traveled along unbeaten paths. He reached his destination by nightfall the next day, without incident.

That's when problems began. The guard at the outpost refused to take him to General Jesup. "I believe you came from the Seminoles," the guard said.

Hungry and exhausted, not having slept or eaten for nearly two days, Beckwourth managed to control his temper. Again, he asked the guard to show him to Jesup. They argued until the guard finally announced his arrival, but he told the general, "Here is another of those Seminoles, sir, who says he has dispatches for you. What shall I do with him?"

Beckwourth was furious. Without knowing anything about Jim except his outward appearance, the guard had accused him of lying.

When Jesup took the messages and disappeared into his tent without even inviting Jim to dismount, Beckwourth turned his horse to leave. Just then Jesup called to him: "Captain Beckwourth, alight! alight, sir, and come into my quarters." Once he'd read the messages, Jesup's attitude changed. He ordered the guard to take care of Beckwourth's horse and, finally, gave Jim a bed and a meal.

At first, Beckwourth and the mountain men saw no fighting. They were stationed at Fort Brooke in Tampa, breaking in mules. Matters changed when they were placed under the command of Colonel Zachary Taylor (who later became president of the United States). Colonel Taylor was not popular with the Missourians. They complained that he and his staff treated them badly and didn't pay as promised.

The muleteers joined army troops moving from the Peace River to the Kissimmee River, building forts every twenty-five miles and putting up bridges and causeways through the marshland between the rivers. Then, on December 24, 1837, Colonel Taylor ordered his troops to move against a large party of Seminoles. They were led by Coa-coo-chee (Wild Cat), who had recently escaped from an army prison.

Coa-coo-chee had stationed his warriors on a hummock overlooking the swamp, about twenty miles from the mouth of Lake Okeechobee.

Taylor wanted to attack them head-on. He ridiculed Gentry, who advised coming at them from the sides instead. At noon on Christmas Day, Beckwourth and his frontiersmen were at the front of Taylor's advance,

Coa-coo-chee, or Wild Cat *(right)*, and his warriors stood up to a U.S. attack on their camp on Christmas Day 1837. Beckwourth admired the Seminoles' bravery as well as their skillful fighting.

along with the Missouri Volunteers and Morgan's Spies. Led by Gentry, they entered the densely wooded area, pushing slowly through the overgrowth and swamp mud. As they drew near the hummock, rifles cracked. Bullets whizzed. From their cover, the Seminoles hollered as they poured volley after volley of rifle fire, aimed with deadly accuracy, into the line of Missourians. Beckwourth, impressed with the Seminoles' fighting skill and spirit, said their yells were the most deafening he'd ever heard.

Stationed in the rear, the regular soldiers fired back, sometimes accidentally shooting into the volunteers. Some of the Missourians gave up and fled. Others stayed and fought. Beckwourth stayed, ducking behind a tree as men died around him. Gentry and several other respected officers were killed.

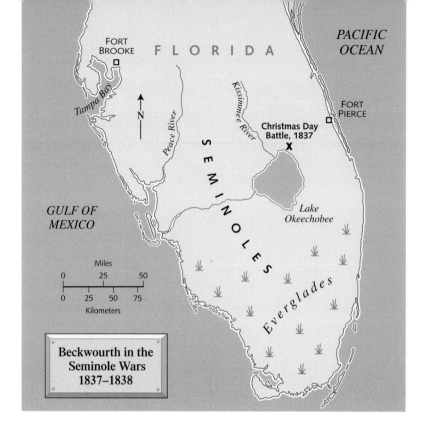

The map shows:
FORT BROOKE
FLORIDA
PACIFIC OCEAN
Tampa Bay
N
Peace River
Kissimmee River
FORT PIERCE
Christmas Day Battle, 1837 X
SEMINOLES
GULF OF MEXICO
Lake Okeechobee
Everglades
Miles
0   25   50
0   25   50   75
Kilometers
Beckwourth in the Seminole Wars 1837–1838

The battle raged for four hours, until the Seminoles withdrew into the swamps. The army suffered terrible losses, with 26 killed and 112 wounded. Beckwourth, along with other Missourians, noted bitterly that they did not see Colonel Taylor in the battle.

As summer grew closer, Jim tired of Florida, with its oppressive heat and annoying mosquitoes. Aside from carrying an occasional dispatch, there was little for him to do. He looked for ways to amuse himself.

One day Beckwourth and the muleteers were accompanying army officers on a trip from Fort Basinger to Tampa Bay. There was no danger of Indian attacks. The major in charge told the muleteers that the officers wanted to ride ahead so they could arrive at Tampa Bay that same day. He gave the muleteers permission to get in the next day, at their leisure.

The men took the offer of leisure as a challenge. "If you can get in to-day, we can." they said. It was an unfair contest. The officers had the best horses, while the muleteers had both slower mounts and pack mules.

They started off together. The officers quickly outpaced the troops, leaving them to pick their way through swamps so difficult that many horses lost their footing. Once on dry land, Beckwourth took the saddle off his mule, wrung out the saddle blanket, and set it in the sun to dry. The other men did likewise, and everyone had a good lunch and a good rest.

Saddled and on the road again, they quickly caught up to the major's party. The officers were toiling slowly, vainly spurring their tired animals to go faster. Beckwourth and his men passed them with a cheer and broke into a gallop a short way from the fort. They had time to have drinks before the officers arrived. Beckwourth relished the victory, explaining that they had won the race by taking care of their animals. "A horse . . . is only flesh and blood," he said.

But the occasional amusements and dispatches did not make up for the long periods of inactivity that Jim hated. Florida seemed to him "a poor field to work in for *renown*." He wanted excitement. After ten months in Florida, Beckwourth and his company were ready to go home.

CHAPTER SEVEN
TRADER, HORSE THIEF, AND SCOUT

NEW MEXICO

Jim rode the steamboat home to Missouri on the Fourth of July 1838, "amid much noise, revelry, and drunken patriotism." After just five days in Saint Louis, he agreed to help two of his friends, Louis Vasquez and Andrew Sublette (the brother of Beckwourth's old friend William Sublette), start a new company to trade with Native Americans in the Southwest. He looked forward to plenty of the excitement he'd missed in Florida. He'd be trading with the Cheyennes, Arapahos, and Sioux, all enemies of the Crows.

First, the company needed a place to trade. Jim joined a crew that was building a new fort on the south fork of the Platte River. One of the workers approached Sublette and asked why he had brought "such a rascally fellow" as Beckwourth.

Over the years, Beckwourth had acquired the reputation of being rough and dishonest. Some of it was justified—he was very good at horse stealing, which was a way to survive among the Crows. Like most frontiersmen, he would lie, fight, or kill when he needed to—and sometimes even when he didn't. However, much of the reputation was unfair and probably stemmed from racism against both black and Native American people. Beckwourth was no more of a ruffian, thief, or liar than most mountain men. He was honest in his business practices and brought a sense of fairness to his dealings with everyone, regardless of their race.

The man complaining to Sublette accused Beckwourth of planning to provoke Native Americans into killing whites. Jim called the accusations "foul reports" and said they were "like stabs in the dark" since no one made the accusations to his face. Sublette defended Beckwourth and put Jim in charge of the fort.

Beckwourth promptly built smaller trading posts throughout the territory. The new company had plenty of supplies and outposts but no customers. Beckwourth sent three different messengers to invite Native Americans to trade. Each messenger returned unable to find any. Frustrated, Jim saddled his own horse and set out with a couple of companions. When he saw buffalo running in small herds, he knew they'd been chased by Native American hunters. That night he saw their campfires, and the next morning, the traders entered the Cheyennes' camp.

Also there to trade was William Bent, a friendly competitor. Bent knew Beckwourth had lived with the Crows and was aghast to see him among the

Cheyennes. "Don't you know that they will kill you
if they discover you?" he asked.

Jim wasn't worried. He let the Cheyennes know
that he was a Crow and admitted killing many of their
people in battle. The Cheyennes respected his
courage. One of the elders said, "We like a great
brave, and we will not kill you; you shall live."

Beckwourth promised to trade fairly. With that, he
and the Cheyennes started sharing war stories. As
they reminisced, one of Jim's companions brought a
ten-gallon keg of whiskey to sell.

Until then, Jim had refused to sell liquor to Native
Americans. Although the Crows did not drink alcohol, many tribes did. Government officials and white
traders gave alcohol to Native Americans to make

Traders at a Native American camp during the 1800s. Some
traders used alcohol to lure Indians into unfair deals. Beckwourth
refused to allow drinking while deals were being struck.

them drunk and then lead them into unfair deals. Liquor became such a big part of dealings between whites and Native Americans that any trader not using it would go out of business.

Beckwourth called the trade in liquor an evil practice. He pointed out that traders made outrageous profits, taking in thousands of dollars worth of buffalo robes from Native Americans for the sale of pennies worth of liquor. He drew a connection between those profits and the extinction of the bison, which were being hunted so heavily that herds were disappearing. Even Native Americans, he said, were calling buffalo hides "a pint of whiskey." But he needed to stay in business too. That day with the Cheyennes, the entire keg was gone within two hours. The Cheyennes agreed to do business with him.

Although he had to trade liquor, Beckwourth adopted his own set of rules to make it less harmful. He insisted that the women trade before he passed out drinks, so that the men could not give away all the robes. He refused to give liquor for credit. He allowed drinking only if it did not interfere with business or with him, and to make sure of this, he insisted that people drink outside of the lodge.

He also knew that cheating Native Americans was not only wrong, it was also bad for business. He'd heard of Native Americans who became so angry that they killed traders who acted unfairly. So, when one Cheyenne chief complained that he had given Beckwourth all his robes for only liquor, Beckwourth immediately welcomed him and his wife to the fort, gave them a feast, and piled up gifts for them—blankets, kettles, and beads, as well as two horses. The chief was so pleased that he became a regular client and a friend.

Jim's business success, however, came from more than his caution in trading liquor. It also came from his deep understanding of Native American culture and his insistence on fairness. As he explained it, "[T]he Indians knew that the whites cheated them, and knew that they could believe what I said. Besides that . . . I had lived so much among them that I could enter into their feelings, and be in every respect one of themselves."

Beckwourth traded along the Arkansas River for three years, long enough to gather new stories and friendships, especially among the Cheyennes. He also earned enough money to go into business for himself. Heading out for new territory, Beckwourth and his friend Charles Towne rode over the rugged passes into Taos, in present-day New Mexico.

Jim opened a store and settled down. He married a new wife, Louise Sandeville (sometimes written as Luisa Sandoval). It is unclear whether they were legally married, since frontiersmen did not always follow the formal rules of marriage. However, it was clearly Jim's first marriage outside of Absaroke. If he missed Pine Leaf or any of his other Crow wives, he didn't mention it. But apparently, he did miss the wilderness. In October 1842, after about a year in Taos, Beckwourth moved back to the frontier along the Arkansas River with Louise and opened another

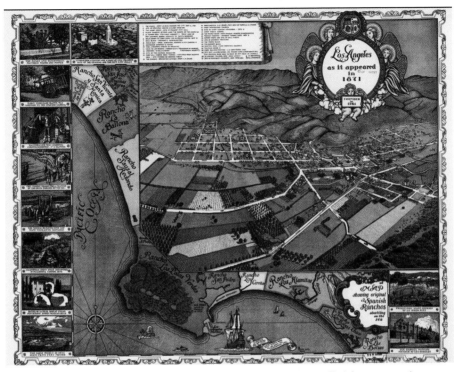

This map shows the growing city of Los Angeles, California, in the mid to late 1800s. Beckwourth called it Pueblo de Angeles and set out for the city in the 1840s.

trading post. It didn't take long for other trappers to join them, creating a settlement that became known as Pueblo, in present-day Colorado.

In the 1840s, tensions were growing between the United States and Mexico. The western part of what was to be Colorado, as well as Texas, California, and much of the Southwest were part of Mexico then. American traders like Beckwourth became unpopular. Jim packed up the goods he hadn't sold, and leaving behind his wife and infant daughter, he took his new passion for trade to what he called Pueblo de Angeles (Los Angeles), California.

He arrived in January 1844. For roughly a year, he did business happily and peacefully. He was impressed with the success of a country free of war, with no costly armies to support.

Peace did not last. Mexico appointed an unpopular California governor, Manuel Micheltorena. He brought with him an army of bandits to enforce laws the Californians thought were unfair. Beckwourth agreed with the Californians and joined a rebellion against the governor. For two days—February 19 and 20, 1845—Beckwourth fought at the Battle of Cahuenga, in the San Fernando Valley north of Los Angeles, to bring down Micheltorena.

During this time, war had broken out between the United States and Mexico. The atmosphere in California grew too tense for Beckwourth. He decided to go back to Pueblo in Colorado. Riding east with five friends, they stole about eighteen hundred "stray" horses along the way.

Taking horses from other tribes was necessary for survival among Native Americans, and the Crows solved arguments among themselves by taking each other's horses. But white society saw horse stealing as a crime. Living in both worlds, Jim seemed to follow a personal code that sometimes reflected the Native American's views, sometimes white society's, and sometimes his own unique morality. In his writings, Jim justified the theft, saying it was wartime. He used the horses in trade with the U.S. Army.

In Pueblo, Beckwourth found to his surprise that Louise, thinking he'd abandoned her, had married someone else. Jim wasn't particularly disappointed. When Louise offered to come back to him, he said no. He was happy to think of himself as single again.

The Mexican-American War (1846–1848) gave Beckwourth the chance to return to the job he always enjoyed, carrying dispatches for the army. At the same time, he and a partner opened a hotel and bar in Santa Fe, New Mexico. Popular with officers and mountaineers, it was described by one visitor as a "grand resort" for drinking, card playing, and dancing.

Using the hotel as his home base, Beckwourth carried messages between Santa Fe and Fort Leavenworth, in present-day Kansas. The nine-hundred-mile journey one way usually took him about twenty-five days. "I well knew that my life was at stake every trip that I made," he recalled, "but I liked the employment;

In this painting, U.S. and Mexican forces fight during the Mexican-American War in 1847. Beckwourth served as a messenger with the U.S. Army during the war.

there was continual excitement in it, indeed, sometimes more than I actually cared [for]."

Excitement came to his home too. Jim was in his hotel on the night of January 19, 1847, when his friend Charles Towne pounded violently on the door. He told Jim about a massacre in Taos. Mexicans and Native Americans had killed nearly all the white people in town. Beckwourth joined about four hundred men on a march to Taos. The old warrior was shocked at the barbarity he found. The streets were littered with tortured bodies. Jim and his companions had known a few of the dead. Beckwourth joined the hunt for the killers.

While in the Santa Fe area, Beckwourth was again falsely accused of conspiring with Native Americans against whites. Rewards were offered for his capture. Friends told him to escape, but Jim wanted to turn himself in and collect the money since he had nothing to hide.

Instead, Lieutenant Colonel David Willock convinced him to join an army expedition against the Apaches as a spy, interpreter, and guide. Apaches had recently killed his friend Charles Towne, so Beckwourth probably felt little affection for the tribe at that time. He went willingly.

The first night out, Jim took one look at the food spread out for the soldiers and decided he wanted more. He told Willock he was going to hunt for an antelope. The colonel was surprised. His soldiers had just scoured the countryside and hadn't found an antelope anywhere. As Jim picked up his rifle to head out anyway, the colonel offered to join him and promised to carry on his own back whatever Beckwourth managed to kill.

Jim liked that deal. Within a half mile, he saw antelope tracks that the colonel missed. He decided to play a trick. Without mentioning the tracks, Jim walked on a bit farther, then stopped, threw his head back, and sniffed the air like a dog. "I am sure that I smell an antelope," he said. The colonel tried sniffing too but could smell nothing.

"Well, colonel," said Jim, "there are antelopes close by, I know, for my smeller's never yet deceived me."

He suggested the colonel go up one hill while he went up another where he knew the antelopes would be. He found them and shot. The colonel was astonished. "And you smelled them!" he said. Although Jim reminded him of his promise to carry the antelope on his back, the colonel arranged instead to have one of his men bring in the game.

The expedition found no Apaches. After reporting back to Fort Laramie, Beckwourth spent many more months carrying dispatches over dangerous ground. He was so successful that newspapers reported on his rides. In late August 1848, he carried his last dispatch for the army from Fort Leavenworth back to California, where gold had just been discovered.

CHAPTER EIGHT
HERE IS
YOUR KINGDOM

CALIFORNIA

"Gold! Gold! Gold from the American River!"

These cries started the gold rush in California in May 1848. From all over the world, people raced to the foothills of California's stark Sierra Nevada to search for treasure.

Most came over land from the East, traveling over the Rockies and the Sierras along the dangerous trails Jim Beckwourth knew so well. The emigrants, as they were called, did not fully understand those dangers. Many died along the way, from disease, accidents, or violence. Some perished of starvation on the frozen slopes of the high Sierras. Everyone who made the trip suffered terribly over steep, nearly impassable routes.

In the early days of the gold rush, Beckwourth worked for the very first regular mail system on the West Coast. Twice a month, riders carried mail in a

Gold fever swept the United States during the mid-1800s. News of gold discoveries, which this pamphlet advertises, drew many people west to California. Beckwourth left the hard work of prospecting to younger men and ran a store in Sonora, a mining town in California's Sierra Nevada.

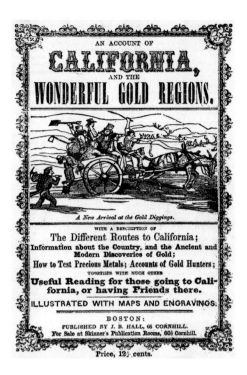

AN ACCOUNT OF

CALIFORNIA,
AND THE
WONDERFUL GOLD REGIONS.

A New Arrival at the Gold Diggings.

WITH A DESCRIPTION OF

The Different Routes to California;
Information about the Country, and the Ancient and Modern Discoveries of Gold;
How to Test Precious Metals; Accounts of Gold Hunters;
TOGETHER WITH MUCH OTHER
Useful Reading for those going to California, or having Friends there.
ILLUSTRATED WITH MAPS AND ENGRAVINGS.

BOSTON:
PUBLISHED BY J. B. HALL, 66 CORNHILL.
For Sale at Skinner's Publication Rooms, 60½ Cornhill.

Price, 12½ cents.

five-hundred-mile relay from San Francisco to San Diego. Jim covered the section from Monterey to Dana's Ranch, north of Santa Barbara. It was a pleasant trip, easy enough for an old mountain man. He made it more pleasant by stopping regularly to visit friends at Mission San Miguel along the way. The family who lived there—William Reed, his wife, Maria Antonia Vallejo, their three-year-old son, and their relatives and servants—were known for their kind hospitality.

So Beckwourth was surprised that no one came out to greet him when he stopped there at dusk in December 1848. Entering the house, he found to his horror that the entire family had been murdered. He raced to his supervisor, Lieutenant (later General) William T. Sherman, breathlessly reporting, "[T]hey killed them all, not even sparing the baby." Sherman's soldiers captured the murderers. Before they were executed, one of them admitted that they were trying to steal the family's gold.

The murder of his friends deeply upset Beckwourth. The sight of an innocent family slaughtered in their own home must have been a painful reminder of the time he'd found his childhood playmates massacred. He called the murder "the most diabolical [evil] deed that ever disgraced the annals [historic records] of frontier life."

He continued carrying mail a few more months, until he could no longer resist the lure of the gold rush. In April 1849, he moved to Sonora, a town known for rich mines, busy stores, and plenty of gambling. Beckwourth opened a store in a tent and soon moved to a roomy house. He did his share of gambling too, becoming known as one of the best card dealers in the area.

He also went into prospecting. Mining was much like trapping—bone hard work requiring long hours in icy water, handling heavy loads. But in his fifties and plagued with the stiff joints of rheumatism, Jim chose to let others do the hard labor. He hired Native Americans and paid them half the earnings they brought in. The arrangement proved to be too quiet for Beckwourth. The "inactivity," he said, "fatigued me to death." He sold his business and, with full pockets, set out for the city of Sacramento. But the money didn't stay in his pockets long.

In the late summer of 1849, Beckwourth stopped at a store upriver from Sacramento. He told the owner,

John Letts, that he was dead broke and hungry. Letts had heard of Beckwourth from a friend who called Jim the best horse thief in New Mexico. Letts gave Beckwourth food. In return, Beckwourth told his life story. Letts called it an "exciting romance, interspersed with thrilling adventures and 'hair-breadth 'scapes.'" One of those "hair-breadth 'scapes'" was the ninety-five-mile race Beckwourth had run years before to escape the Blackfeet, which gave his legs the look, Letts said, "of being bound with cords under the skin, [because] of the general rupture of the blood vessels."

Beckwourth returned to Letts's store some days later, flying up at a wild gallop and letting out a loud whoop. He burst in, threw a handkerchief filled with coins onto the counter, and announced, "Well, I vow, captain, I've made a raise." Then he untied the handkerchief to display the gold and silver inside. He insisted Letts keep the silver, half of his winnings from gambling. He took the rest with him to Sacramento, where he spent it all buying drinks and entertainment for the town.

Beckwourth moved back to the Sierra foothills that fall, and the next spring, 1850, he went on a mining expedition. He and a friend rode north, into Pit River country, crossing over high mountains. They didn't find anything worth mining, but from the heights, Beckwourth saw "a place far away to the southward that seemed lower than any other." Since it was lower, it would be warmer than the surrounding areas. That meant there might be an easier pass there for people traveling in wagons over the Sierras into California. Beckwourth knew that an easier pass could be worth more than gold. But first, he had to find it. At the end of April, he returned to the area with a dozen men. All of them were searching for gold, except Jim. He was searching for his pass.

They entered a green valley dotted with flowers of every color, filled with birds and their songs. Geese and ducks sailed across the surface of the cool streams or flew through the clouds above them. The boldness of the deer and antelope convinced Jim that no hunter had visited the valley before them. He suspected that he and his companions were the first non-Native Americans to walk that land.

Beckwourth in the mid-1800s, about the time he discovered a pass through the Sierra Nevada. This illustration is from a book and a magazine story published about him during the same period.

On the other side of the beautiful valley, they followed the Yuba River to the Truckee River, where the waters flowed eastward. Jim realized they had traveled without trouble from the western to the eastern slope of the Sierras. He had found his pass! The others also found a little gold, but not enough to bother trying to mine. Beckwourth's discovery was much more valuable.

He told people at American Ranch and other nearby communities about his idea to create a road and collected hundreds of dollars from investors for the work. He met with the mayor of the largest neighboring city, Marysville, which would be the main stop for newcomers seeking to build homes and start businesses. The mayor was excited. He predicted that Jim's investors would earn thousands. He promised to repay Jim for the cost of building the road.

Beckwourth set a crew to work clearing the route while he went back to the Truckee River to lead travelers to the new pass. Before he could find anyone, he fell ill. Weak, feverish, and more than one hundred miles from help, he huddled into a shelter of brush by the Truckee River, wrote a will, and prepared to die.

It was August 1851. The short Sierra summer was already turning into the chill of fall. While Jim shivered with fever, a train of seventeen wagons pulled up nearby to make camp. The animals were thin and sickly. The people were dirty, sunburned, exhausted, worried about a possible attack by Native Americans, and afraid of the steep mountains in front of them.

Jim gathered enough strength to leave his shelter and tell the travelers about the pass. They agreed to try it if he could guide them to it. With care from the women on the train—"God bless them!" said Jim— he recovered enough in a few days to ride again.

One of the passengers was ten-year-old Ina Smith, who later became well known as Ina Coolbrith, a California poet. Fascinated by the stories Jim told after supper every night, she thought he was "one of the most beautiful creatures that ever lived," with his dark skin, his two long braids tied with colored cords, his leather coat and moccasins.

Jim rode bareback in front of the train as they traveled for three days over ground no wagon had traveled before. When they reached the pass, he wheeled his horse around to find Ina's mother and ask if her daughters would like to ride into California with him. "I was the happiest little girl in the world," Ina said. He lifted Ina and her sister in front of him, and they rode to the border of California. There, he stopped, pointed, and said, "Here in California, little girls, here is your kingdom." With that, the old mountain man and the little girls led the first wagon train through what would soon be known as the Beckwourth Pass.

The people of Marysville turned out to celebrate the successful journey. Unfortunately, things got out of hand. A fire broke out that night, leaving much of the town in ashes. When the Marysville mayor congratulated Jim for bringing the train safely through, he also said the town could no longer afford to pay Jim's costs

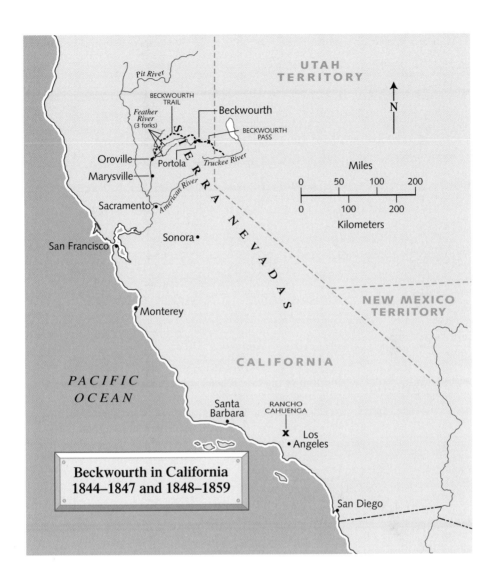

Beckwourth in California
1844–1847 and 1848–1859

as promised. Jim applied for his money repeatedly over the next few years, but the city always turned him down. "Sixteen hundred dollars I expended upon the road is forever gone," Jim wrote angrily, "but those who derive advantage from this outlay and loss of time devote no thought to the discoverer."

Marysville certainly did benefit from the pass. Many thousands came through during its peak years of use, 1851 through 1855.

Jim spent that fall on the North Fork of Rio de las Plumas (Feather River), near the Sierra foothill community of Rich Bar. Well known as a mountain man and discoverer of the Beckwourth Pass, he quickly earned a reputation as a storyteller too. One letter-writer, known as Dame Shirley, described him to her sister back East: "He is fifty years of age, perhaps, and speaks several languages to perfection. . . . He chills the blood of the green young miner[s] . . . by the cold blooded manner in which he relates the Indian fights that he has been engaged in."

Cold-blooded though he may have seemed, Beckwourth talked a group of Native Americans out of a murderous attack on the miners Dame Shirley continued to describe. The old warrior was learning to create peace.

By the following spring, 1852, Jim was back in his beautiful valley by the Beckwourth Pass. He built a cabin, called it the War Horse Ranch, and settled down as a "hotel-keeper and chief of a trading-post." Two streams raced through his valley, sending out small branches that irrigated the rich soil. Fish, game, fowl, and wild cherries flourished. Jim raised cattle and planted a kitchen garden where he grew cabbages, turnips, and radishes "of great size." The weather was far gentler there than on the surrounding peaks, and the snowmelt from the higher elevations kept icy water flowing even during the summer.

For years, Jim's War Horse Ranch was the first hostel available to travelers coming to California over Beckwourth Pass. Jim was proud of the "refreshing

Researchers believe this cabin in California to be part of Beckwourth's War Horse Ranch, where he gave shelter and food to travelers and told his life story to writer T. D. Bonner. It is now open to visitors as the Beckwourth Museum.

repose [rest]" it gave settlers. As he watched exhausted families straggle in hungry and broke, he remembered his own early experiences in the wilderness. It was his chance to keep the vow he'd made after eating the teal duck while his companions were starving. He shared whatever he could with the emigrants, freely giving them food and graze for their horses. Most of the settlers promised to pay him, but many never did. Still, he kept giving. He could not turn down a traveler in need. He said, "If my pocket suffers a little, I have my recompense [payment] in a feeling of internal satisfaction."

He also had the satisfaction of an eager audience. Many settlers made notes in their diaries about Jim's stories. When the travelers took out their guitars and fiddles, there would be a merry night around the campfire at the War Horse Ranch. And if travelers arrived missing a few horses that had been stolen along the way, Jim was ready to head up a party to retrieve them.

In the fall of 1854, T. D. Bonner showed up at Jim's ranch. Bonner was a newspaper writer who joined the gold rush and worked as a justice of the peace in a nearby town. He knew a good story when he heard one. In October, he and Beckwourth filed a contract in Plumas County agreeing that Bonner would write Beckwourth's autobiography, publish it in a pamphlet, and share the profits equally with Jim.

The men spent that winter and much of 1855 in Beckwourth's cabin. Jim spun his tale, and T.D. wrote it "literally as it was from day to day related." Rumors went around about the high times they had—the more rum they drank, it was said, the more fantastic Jim's stories grew. "Paint her up, Bonner!" Jim was quoted as saying as he slapped the writer's knee, telling Bonner to exaggerate the stories to make them even more exciting. "Paint her up!"

It didn't take long for them to realize that Jim's life was too big for a pamphlet. In November the two men signed another contract, this time for a book. After he'd written all Beckwourth had to tell, Bonner sold the story to an East Coast publisher. He didn't earn much money on it, and Jim never saw a cent.

What Jim did see from the book, and also from the people traveling over his pass, was plenty of the renown he'd sought for so long. But fame didn't seem to change the way he lived. He still could not stay settled. After seven years on his ranch, Jim Beckwourth lit out again, heading home to Saint Louis one last time.

CHAPTER NINE

A POLISHED GENTLEMAN

COLORADO

The man who could blaze his way through pathless wilderness got lost in the streets of Saint Louis the spring of 1859. The city had changed so completely that Jim had to hire a guide to lead him to his brother's house.

Uncomfortable in the unfamiliar city, he left quickly, planning to guide a wagon train west, spend the winter visiting the Crows, then return to his California ranch. His plans changed when his horse threw him the day he was scheduled to leave. Fortunately, his injuries weren't serious, and he soon signed up with his old friend, Louis Vasquez, to take a wagon train of supplies to Vasquez's store in Denver.

He made the trip to Denver in early October, passing through Cheyenne country in the Great Plains. It had been ten years since he had traded among them. Still, the Cheyennes recognized Beckwourth and welcomed him warmly. But a less welcoming sight greeted him along the way—white settlers putting up towns in what had once been hunting grounds. Beckwourth understood the threat those villages posed to the Native American way of life.

In November he told a newspaper editor, William Byers of Denver's *Rocky Mountain News,* that he wanted to put a stop to settlers crowding the open spaces. Beckwourth was famous by then, and Byers welcomed him with both interest and surprise. Byers had expected "a rough, illiterate back-woodsman," but instead found Jim "a polished gentleman, possessing a fund of general information which few can boast."

This illustration shows Beckwourth in fine city clothes. It was created about the time he settled down to be a merchant in west Denver.

Beckwourth set to work immediately managing Vasquez's store on Ferry Street in west Denver (then known as Auraria). The shop catered to the needs of Denver's pioneers. Along with groceries, candles, and winter clothing, Jim sold nails, window glass, glass dishes, champagne and wine, and an assortment of fine china. An ad for the store in the *Rocky Mountain News* pointed out that there was "no longer any necessity of eating out of tin."

Many Native Americans came to the store, too, for goods and also for Jim's help with white people. Beckwourth tried to explain the Native Americans' viewpoint to whites by bringing their concerns to Byers, who published them in his newspaper. Although the paper published Beckwourth's articles in support of the Native Americans, it also led a campaign of hatred against them.

In one case, Beckwourth told of meeting several Cheyennes who had recently arrived in town hungry. They pointed out that Cheyennes never failed to feed white people lost on Cheyenne land, yet no one in Denver offered them any help. Jim gave them a hearty meal at his store.

More troubling incidents came to Beckwourth's attention as well. Calling for "Justice to the Indians," he wrote about a vicious attack by white thugs—he called them "drunken devils" and "bummers"—on a group of Cheyennes and Apaches who had come to Denver to trade. Led by a man known as Big Phil the Cannibal, the whites sneaked into the group's campsite after dark, while the men were away, and attacked the women. The white men stole three mules as they left.

In his letter to the newspaper, Beckwourth said the Native Americans were as hurt by the injustice as they were eager for revenge. They felt the wrong even more, he said, because it was done "*upon their own lands*, which they have been deprived of, their game driven off and they made to suffer by hunger, and when they pay a visit, [they are] abused more than the dogs."

Public meetings and investigations followed Beckwourth's letter, leading to his appointment as the local agent of Native American affairs. It became his job to take care of Native Americans during their visits to Denver, to keep track of crimes committed by either side against the other, and to conduct all local business with them. Beckwourth took his responsibilities very seriously. With his new authority, he repeated his old calls for white people to stop using liquor to cheat Native Americans.

On June 21, 1860, Jim married again. He had not forgotten his earlier wives—he had recently dedicated his autobiography to Pine Leaf and said he longed to return to both her and Nom-ne-dit-chee. But they were not in Denver—Elizabeth Ledbetter was.

Very little is known about Elizabeth, although she was said to be attractive. The newspapers publicly announced their marriage. Jim's devotion to her was noted even by an agent in a shipping office, who said he was "the very pink of courtesy, and specially devoted to a comely young wife whom he invariably dignifies with the title of 'Lady Beckwourth.'"

The two moved a short distance south of Denver, to land along the South Platte River owned by Vasquez. They grew corn, potatoes, pumpkins, melons, and vegetables along a bend in the river. Within a few months, they moved to their own farm about a mile south along the South Platte. Not long after, they had a baby girl and named her Julia, the last of Beckwourth's known children. Although he probably had many children, historians know for certain of only three.

Now Jim had fame, family, and property. He paid taxes and ran a business. James Pierson Beckwourth had become a respectable citizen. He was so well regarded that, when Vasquez decided to go out of business, he put Jim in charge of keeping track of the money and goods. Beckwourth's old friend, the famous mountain man Jim Bridger, also asked him to take care of property that he owned in Denver.

Bridger and Beckwourth had kept in touch throughout the years. In December 1861, Bridger wrote to Beckwourth from Missouri. It was the first year of the Civil War (1861–1865), and Bridger, who could not spell correctly, reported, "the hole country is up side down here." He said that ever since Abraham Lincoln had been elected president, Southern states had quit the union (left the United States) and had no government to take charge.

As the Civil War started to stir up the country, Beckwourth's old longings started to stir inside him.

Respectability did not provide the freedom or challenges he loved. He left for a while during 1862 to work as an army guide with the Colorado Second Infantry. He returned, but he had a hard time following the rules of city life and marriage. In February 1863, he was charged with stealing a saddle, bridle, and blankets from the army. The charges were dropped, but they signaled change.

A little more than a year later, tragedy stuck. On April 29, 1864, at five thirty in the morning, baby Julia died at the age of one year, eight months, and eight days. Jim and Elizabeth's marriage was beginning to die too.

Then came another legal accusation, this time for manslaughter. On a Saturday night just two weeks after Julia's death, Bill Payne, a blacksmith known as "a savage and dangerous character," came to the Beckwourths' home. He tried to force a ring off Elizabeth's finger. Her cries awoke Jim, who was ill and in bed. In the course of the fight that followed, Beckwourth shot and killed Payne. His trial was set for August.

In the meantime, Jim and Elizabeth took steps to end their marriage by selling property they owned together. Soon Jim was living with another woman, a Native American known as Sue. They lived a mountaineer's life at the farm, with Jim setting traps in the mornings and Sue skinning the animals and treating the hides later in the day. Friendly Native Americans set up tents around their home, creating the kind of frontier community where Jim felt comfortable.

On August 13, 1864, the jury in Beckwourth's manslaughter trial heard the testimony of the witnesses. It took them only a few minutes to declare him not guilty. He went on his way rejoicing and free.

CHAPTER TEN
THE SAND CREEK MASSACRE

COLORADO

While Jim and Sue were living peacefully outside Denver, Colorado, the Civil War was spreading chaos across the country. The government pulled army troops away from forts in the West to fight in the East. In their absence, some Native Americans, forced out of their homelands and sometimes into starvation by whites, burned down empty forts and attacked white settlers. Soldiers who remained in the West sometimes killed innocent Native Americans, leading to more raids against whites. A false report spread that the tribes were going to rise up together to slaughter all whites.

White people in Colorado were in a panic over that rumor and others, both true and false, about Native American crimes against whites. In response, the governor formed the Third Regiment of Volunteer Cavalry, headquartered in Denver, to put a stop to the

This broadside (ad) from 1864 urges men to join the cavalry (a branch of the U.S. military that fought from horseback) to fight Indians. In addition to pay, food, and plunder, volunteers were offered a fixed, one-hundred-day term of service.

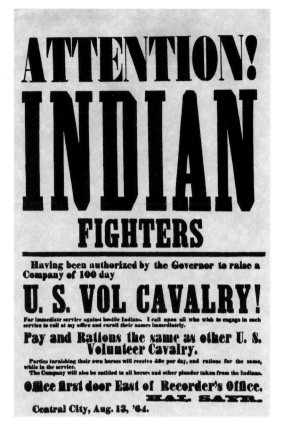

Native American raids. It was to be in business for one hundred days, so its men were called "hundred-dazers." They were under the command of Colonel John Chivington, a large, burly officer who had been a Methodist minister and who wanted to kill all the local Native American tribes.

To drum up volunteers, posters were put up, war meetings were held, speeches were made. Too few men came forward, so on August 23, 1864, Chivington ordered a state of martial law to urge more men to sign up. That meant businesses had to close, and no trains or wagons were allowed to leave the territory.

The regiment needed a guide and interpreter—Jim Beckwourth's kind of job. This time Jim did not want to do it. He said he was forced to sign up under a threat against his life. As a black man during the Civil War, he was in a difficult position. Even in the North, racism was common, and blacks were subject to harsher treatment than whites in the Union army. If captured by the Confederates in the South, black men would be enslaved or possibly even executed. Justifiably concerned for his own safety, Beckwourth agreed to help, even though he wanted no part in Chivington's plan.

On November 21, Beckwourth arrived at the army's camp along the Arkansas River to help guide the hundred-dazers on a march east, looking for Native Americans. They were heading for Fort Lyon in Colorado.

The Native Americans camped near the fort were peaceful Cheyennes and Arapahos. They included followers of Cheyenne chief Black Kettle, who had saved the lives of many white soldiers and pioneers. The groups were settling in for the winter on the bluffs of Sand Creek, with the promise of protection and help from the troops at Fort Lyon.

Over the opposition of his officers, Chivington decided to attack the peaceful settlement. At eight o'clock the night of November 28, 1864, he ordered his men to snuff out their campfires and fall into formation. Jim Beckwourth refused—the cold night air made him too stiff, he said. He waited until daylight, early enough to catch up.

He was at Chivington's side the morning of November 29. They could see ice crusted on the nearly dry river and a horse herd grazing past a scattering of cottonwood and willow trees. Less than a mile to the west, the tents of Cheyennes and Arapahos speckled the bank at the river's bend. Yapping camp dogs and movements among the lodges told the soldiers that the Native Americans had spotted them.

The women were excited, believing the approaching cloud of dust to be a herd of bison. It didn't take long for them to realize the dust was actually made by soldiers, but they were not alarmed. They'd been promised protection.

Then the army began shooting. Beckwourth found himself in the first charge. But whose side was he on? Many of the Cheyennes under attack were his friends from long ago. But he'd always supported the United States, the country his father fought to found, the government that was fighting to end slavery. He'd spent much of his career helping the army. Here the army was committing a massacre he knew was wrong.

Beckwourth felt no joy in this fight. Instead of killing, he turned to saving lives. He put two wounded men onto an ambulance, then brought a Cheyenne woman and another wounded soldier into the safety of camp. He stayed with them.

But not before he saw the murder and mutilation of White Antelope—known to the Cheyennes as Spotted Antelope—who tried to stop the battle. Not before he saw the merciless slaughter of babies, children, women, and elderly people. At camp he witnessed one more crime that day—the murder of Jack Smith, a half-Cheyenne man who had been hired to help Jim.

Fighting and atrocities lasted into the afternoon. When it was over, Chivington's men looted the Native American village and then burned it down. Although many Native Americans survived, including Chief Black Kettle, hundreds of innocent Cheyennes and Arapahos were slaughtered that day.

Cheyennes and Arapahos defend themselves against a U.S. Cavalry charge at Sand Creek near Fort Lyon, Colorado, in 1864. Unprovoked, the cavalry massacred hundreds of people, who had been promised safe residence there. Beckwourth was disgusted.

The army's betrayal of its promised protection led directly to more bloodshed.

Jim Beckwourth, the old warrior, truly had his fill of war. The next January, 1865, his conscience heavy for his role in leading the army to Sand Creek, Jim rode out looking for the Cheyennes, hoping to come to peace with them. They had been on the warpath since the massacre. Jim found them easily. They were on White Man's Fork near Smoky Hill, where militant Natives Americans were known to camp.

One of the chiefs, Leg-in-the-Water, addressed Beckwourth by his Crow name. "Medicine Calf, what have you come here for," he asked, "have you fetched the white man to finish killing our families again?" Beckwourth said he wanted to convince them to make peace, since their numbers were too few to defeat the white people.

"We know it," the Native Americans said, "But what do we want to live for? The white man has taken our country, killed all of our game; was not satisfied with that, but killed our wives and children. . . . We loved the whites until we found out they lied to us, and robbed us of what we had. We have raised the battle-axe until death."

Beckwourth left, but he was not finished trying to make amends. The next spring, he testified against Chivington in military hearings investigating the Sand Creek tragedy. As a result of the investigations, the government condemned the attack. It was called "a foul and dastardly massacre." However, no other action was taken, and Chivington was never punished.

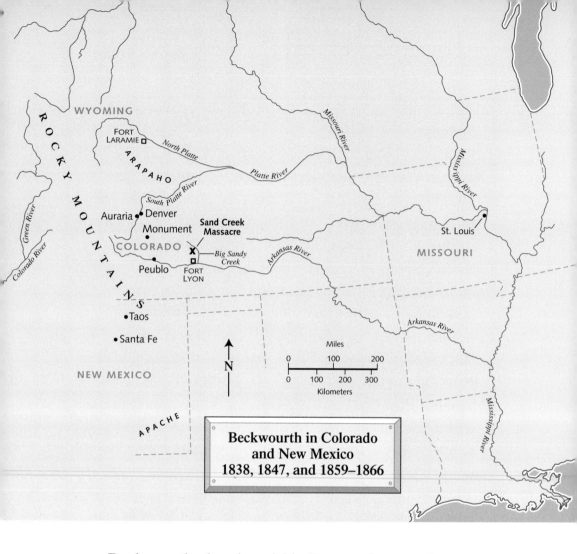

Beckwourth in Colorado
and New Mexico
1838, 1847, and 1859–1866

Beckwourth abandoned his Denver farm and spent the winters of 1865 and 1866 camping in a tent along Monument Creek, a couple of miles south of Monument, Colorado. He tried trapping again in the winter of 1866, taking an expedition to the Green River, where he'd begun so many years before. It ended in disaster. His horses were stolen, and all of his companions were killed. Still, even though he was sixty-eight years old, Jim managed to survive the ordeal by making his way to a settlement to find horses. He brought nearly three hundred pelts with him. The *Rocky Mountain Times* reported that he had "almost material enough for another book of adventures."

Apparently, Beckwourth thought so too. That August, he went to work as a scout for the army at Fort Laramie. A young soldier was surprised to find the old trapper sitting on his bunk: "His knees were pulled up towards him," the soldier said, "and upon them rested many sheets of paper, these supported by a board, forming an improvised desk. He was laboriously writing, or trying to write; anyway it did not seem to come easy. . . . His pistols hanging from the belt were lying on the gray army blanket beside him on the bed. I was looking fixedly at him and wondering who he could be, when suddenly he raised his head and asked: 'Son, is this your bunk?'"

Soon the young man was sitting next to Beckwourth, chatting with him. Jim explained that he was writing another autobiography, which has never been found.

Even the army outpost was too close to civilization for Beckwourth. He soon left, partnering with his old friend Jim Bridger on an army expedition to the Crows. Jim Beckwourth was finally going home to Absaroke.

EPILOGUE

The life of Jim Beckwourth *(left)* made the kind of story that called for legends about his death, and there were many. One said he died being thrown from a horse while on a buffalo hunt with the Crows. Another said the Crows poisoned him when he refused to stay with them as their chief. The most reliable said he grew ill while on his way to the Crow village. The tribe cared for him but could not cure him. At the end of October 1866, James Pierson Beckwourth died and was buried by the Crows.

When he was working with T. D. Bonner on his autobiography, Beckwourth predicted that he might end his days among the Crows. "There at least was fidelity, and when my soul should depart for the spirit land," he said, he hoped the Crows would paint his bones and treasure them so that he could find final rest in his "ever-flowering hunting ground."

BECKWOURTH'S
SIERRA NEVADA LEGACY

Although James Beckwourth's story is not as well-known as that of other frontiersmen, in Plumas County in the Sierra Nevada of northern California, his name is just about everywhere. Past the splashing Feather River is the Beckwourth District Ranger Office, the town of Beckwourth (population 233), Beckwourth Peak (elevation 7,255 feet), and Beckwourth Pass (elevation 5,212 feet).

Markers dot the countryside showing where Beckwourth's trail ran, connecting his pass to what was then the gold mining town of Bidwell's Bar, now the site of Lake Oroville. The trail can be hard to find in places, but some markers follow the paved, well-traveled Highway 70. Each marker describes a portion of the trail, and many markers have diary entries from pioneers who made the journey.

There is also the Beckwourth Museum, which some people believe is the cabin Beckwourth built in 1852 and called his War Horse Ranch. Although there is no way to be certain, it dates from about that period. According to Betty Folchi, the friendly museum director who welcomes visitors, it was built with a V-notch construction typical of cabins in Missouri where Beckwourth grew up. It's a simple, two-room building with a loft. Today it houses items used during Beckwourth's time, such as cookware and boxes of candles. An entire wall is dedicated to photos, articles, and documents about the famous mountain man. Details about the museum can be found at http://www.ci.portola.ca.us/beckwourth_museum.htm.

The Plumas County Museum in the nearby town of Quincy displays more relics, including Jim's stirrups, one of his bullet molds, and samples of his handwriting. In a back room, shelves hold even more treasures, including articles about and by him, diaries written by people who met him, copies of contracts he signed, and fliers from town events celebrating the man and his era.

Beckwourth's Sand Creek Massacre Testimony

In 1865 Beckwourth testified against Colonel John Chivington at military hearings investigating the Sand Creek Massacre. Much of Beckwourth's testimony follows.

The oath being administered according to law, in [the] presence of J. M. Chivington, late colonel first Colorado cavalry, James P. Beckwith testified as follows:

Question: Your full name, age, and residence?

Answer: James Pierson Beckwith. I reside in this city [Denver] at present. I am in my 69th year.

Question: How long have you resided in what is now known as Colorado Territory?

Answer: Off and on for forty-nine years. Not in this Territory that long.

Question: Did you accompany Colonel Chivington's command to Sand [C]reek last November?

Answer: Yes. I started with Colonel Shoup as guide and interpreter; afterwards Colonel Chivington overtook us, and, I think, assumed command.

Question: Were you present at Sand creek at the time of the attack upon Black Kettle's camp, by Colonel Chivington?

Answer: Yes, I was present.

Question: Previous to the attack on Black Kettle's village, did you hear Colonel Chivington give any orders or make any remarks to his command?

Answer: Yes.

Question: What orders did he give, and what remarks did he make to his command?

Answer: His remark, when he halted us in the middle of Sand [C]reek was this: "Men, strip for action." He also said, "I don't tell you to kill all ages and sex, but look back on the plains of the Platte, where your mothers, fathers, brothers, sisters have been slain, and their blood saturating the sands on the Platte. . . ."

Question: At what time in the morning did the attack on Black Kettle commence?

Answer: A little after sunrise.

Question: At what time was the attack over?

Answer: I think it was between 2 and 3 P.M. when they ceased firing. I had not the time of day with me, but guess it was about that time.

Question: Were any Indians killed? If so, state how many.

Answer: It is impossible for me to say how many were killed. A great many were killed, but I cannot guess within a hundred how many were killed.

Question: Were those Indians killed on Sand [C]reek, warriors?

Answer: There were all sexes, warriors, women, and children, and all ages, from one week old up to eighty years.

Question: What proportion of those killed were women and children?

Answer: About two-thirds, as near as I saw.

Question: Were any of the Indians killed at Sand [C]reek scalped, and otherwise mutilated?

Answer: They were scalped; that I know of. White Antelope was the only one I saw that was otherwise mutilated.

Question: Did the Indians at Sand [C]reek, at the time of the attack, form in line of battle to resist Colonel Chivington's command?

Answer: Not until they had been run out of their village.

Question: What did the Indians do at the time of the attack upon them by Colonel Chivington?

Answer: They run out of the village, and formed to fight until the shells were thrown among them, and they broke and fought all over the country.

Commission adjourned until 2 P.M. this day.

****

Question: Did any of the Indians make an attempt to reach Colonel Chivington's command at the time of the attack?

Answer: Yes, one Indian.

Question: Do you know his name? If so, state it, and what he did.

Answer: The name he went by with the Indians was Spotted Antelope, and by the whites, White Antelope. He came running out to meet the command at the time the battle had commenced, holding up his hands and saying "Stop! stop!" He spoke it in as plain English as I can. He stopped and folded his arms until shot down. I don't know whether the colonels heard it or not, as there was such a whooping and hallooing that it was hard to hear what was said.

Question: Was any attention paid to White Antelope as he advanced towards Colonel Chivington's command?

Answer: None, only to shoot him, as I saw.

Question: Did White Antelope have anything in his hand as he advanced towards the command?

Answer: Nothing that I saw.

Question: How near Colonel Chivington's command was White Antelope shot down?

Answer: As near as, I can guess, fifteen or twenty steps.

Question: Was White Antelope scalped and otherwise mutilated?

Answer: Yes, both.

Question: Did you see any person engaged in scalping White Antelope?

Answer: I did not. I saw him, though, after this had been done. . . .

Question: Have you seen any of the Cheyennes since the day of the attack on Sand [C]reek?

Answer: Yes.

Question: When and where did you see them?

Answer: I saw them between the 9th and 12th of January, on the White Man's fork. I went into their village in the night. The White Man's fork heads in the vicinity of the Smoky Hill. It used to be called the Box Elder by the trappers.

Question: How large a village was it?

Answer: There were about one hundred and thirty or one hundred and forty lodges. They were then traveling north.

Question: Were they all Cheyennes?

Answer: No, they were mixed up with other tribes, half-breed Cheyennes, Kiowas, and Camanche warriors. There may have been some Arapahoe lodges among them; most of the lodges were Cheyenne.

Question: Were there any chiefs among them? If so, state who they were.

Answer: There were Leg[s]-in-the-Water, who was then acting as chief, (Black Kettle was not there), and Little Robe, son of the old war chief who was killed at Sand creek. . . .

Question: While in the camp of the Indians on White Man's fork, did you have any conversation with them in reference to Sand creek?

Answer: Yes.

Question: What was said. . . ?

Answer: I went into the lodge of Leg-in-the-Water. When I [w]ent in he raised up and he said, "Medicine Calf, what have you come here for; have you fetched the white man to finish killing our families again?" I told him I had come to talk to him; call in your council. They came in a short time afterwards, and wanted to know what I had come for. I told them I had come to persuade them to make peace with the whites, as there was not enough of them to fight the whites, as they were as numerous as the leaves of the trees. "We know it," was the general response of the council. But what do we want to live for? The white man has taken our country, killed all of our game; was not satisfied with that, but killed our wives and children. Now no peace. We want to go and meet our families in the spirit land. We loved the whites until we found out they lied to us, robbed us of what we had. We have raised the battle-axe until death.

They asked me then why I had come to Sand [C]reek with the soldiers to show them the country. I told them if I had not come the white chief would have hung me. "Go and stay with your white brothers, but we are going to fight till death." I obeyed orders and came back, willing to play quits. There was nothing mentioned about horses or anything that transpired on the battlefield, with the exception of their wives and children. . . .

Source Notes

6   Elinor Wilson, *Jim Beckwourth: Black Mountain Man, War Chief of the Crows, Trader, Trapper, Explorer, Frontiersman, Guide Scout, Interpreter, Adventurer, and Gaudy Liar* (Norman: University of Oklahoma Press, 1972), 6.

6   Ibid., 5.

7   James P. Beckwourth and T. D. Bonner, *The Life and Adventures of James P. Beckwourth: Mountaineer, Scout, and Pioneer, and Chief of the Crow Nation of Indians,* 1856, repr. edited with introduction by Delmont R. Oswald (Lincoln: University of Nebraska Press, 1972), 604.

10   Ibid., 13–14.

10   Ibid., 14.

11   Ibid.

16   Bil Gilbert. The Trailblazers, The Old West (Alexandria, VA: Time-Life Books 1973), 64.

20   Beckwourth, 29.

20   Ibid., 31.

24   Ibid., 37–38.

24   Ibid., 39.

26   Ibid., 64.

30–31   Ibid., 112.

32   Ibid., 104–106.

33   Ibid., 123–124.

34   Ibid., 141.

35   Ibid., 144.

35   Ibid., 179.

40   Ibid., 202.

40–41   Ibid., 205.

42   Ibid., 167.

42   Ibid., 193.

43   Ibid., 195.

44   Ibid., 323.

46   Ibid., 268.

47   Ibid., 361.

48   Ibid., 295.
51   Ibid., 370–371.
51   Ibid., 379–380.
51   Ibid., 384.
53   Ibid., 401.
53   Ibid., 401–402.
57   Ibid., 409–410.
59   Ibid., 413.
60   Ibid.
63   Ibid., 416.
64   Ibid., 417.
64   Ibid., 424.
66   Ibid., 427–428.
68   Ibid., 463.
72   Ibid., 477.
73   Ibid., 491–492.
76   Wilson, 119–120.
76   Beckwourth, 509.
77   Ibid., 515.
80   Ibid., 518.
80   Leslie Stewart, "The Adventures of James Beckwourth," *Sierra Heritage* (September/October 1992), 48.
80   George Wharton James, *Heroes of California: The Story of the Founders of the Golden State as Narrated by Themselves or Gleaned from Other Sources* (Boston: Little, Brown, and Co., 1910), 112.
81   Beckwourth, 519.
82   Wilson, 137.
82   Beckwourth, 526–527.
84   Ibid., 604.
86   Nolie Mumey, *James Pierson Beckwourth, 1856–1866, An Enigmatic Figure of the West: A History of the Latter Years of His Life* (Denver: The Old West Publishing Company, 1957), 53.
87   Ibid., 56.
87   Wilson, 165–166.
89   Mumey, 59.

89 Ibid., 71.
90 Wilson, 174.
97 Mumey, 137–138.
97 Stan Hoig, *The Sand Creek Massacre* (Norman: University of Oklahoma Press, 1987), 291.
99 Mumey, 158–159.
99 Wilson, 181.
100 Beckwourth, 371.

SELECTED BIBLIOGRAPHY

Beckwourth, James P., and T. D. Bonner. *The Life and Adventures of James P. Beckwourth: Mountaineer, Scout, and Pioneer, and Chief of the Crow Nation of Indians.* 1856. Reprint, Lincoln: University of Nebraska Press, 1972.

Chittendon, Hiram Martin. *The American Fur Trade of the Far West.* Vol. 1. Stanford, CA: Academic Reprints, 1954.

Clappe, Louise Amelia Knapp Smith. *The Shirley Letters from the California Mines, 1851–1852.* Berkeley, CA: Heyday Books, 1998.

Dale, Harrison Clifford, ed. *The Ashley-Smith Explorations and the Discovery of a Central Route to the Pacific, 1822–1829.* Cleveland: The Arthur H. Clark Company, 1918.

DeVoto, Bernard. *Across the Wide Missouri.* Boston: Houghton Mifflin, 1947.

Hammond, Andrew. *Following the Beckwourth Trail.* Chico, CA: A. and J. Hammond, 1994.

Hoig, Stan. *The Sand Creek Massacre.* Norman: University of Oklahoma Press, 1987.

Lowie, Robert H. *The Crow Indians.* New York: Holt, Rinehart and Winston, 1956.

Mumey, Nolie. *James Pierson Beckwourth, 1856–1866, An Enigmatic Figure of the West: A History of the Latter Years of His Life.* Denver: The Old West Publishing Company, 1957.

Page, Jake. *In the Hands of the Great Spirit: The 20,000-Year History of American Indians.* New York: Simon & Schuster Inc., 2003.

Stannard, David E. *American Holocaust: Columbus and the Conquest of the New World.* New York: Oxford University Press, 1992.

Wilson, Elinor. *Jim Beckwourth: Black Mountain Man, War Chief of the Crows, Trader, Trapper, Explorer, Frontiersman, Guide Scout, Interpreter, Adventurer, and Gaudy Liar.* Norman: University of Oklahoma Press, 1972.

OTHER RESOURCES

Article

Little, Jane Braxton. "Mystery Cabin—Did Black Pioneer Build It or Not?" *The Sacramento Bee* (December 27, 1995).

Books

Gilbert, Bil. *The Trailblazers.* The Old West. Alexandria, VA: Time-Life Books, 1973.

Katz, William Loren. *Black Indians: A Hidden Heritage.* New York: Aladdin, 1997.

McGraw, Eloise Jarvis. *Moccasin Trail.* New York: Scholastic, 1980.

Websites

Early California History
http://memory.loc.gov/ammem/cbhtml/
Discover information about California history from the first peoples through the middle of the twentieth century.

Mountain Men and the Fur Trade
http://www.xmission.com/~drudy/amm.html
This website is a "research center devoted to the history and traditions of trappers, explorers, and traders known as mountain men."

The Nineteenth Century in Print:
The Making of America in Periodicals.
http://lcweb2.loc.gov/ammem/ndlpcoop/moahtml/snchome.html
Use search term *Beckwourth* to find a period *Harper's Illustrated Weekly Magazine* story about the legendary mountain man.

Northern Cheyenne Sand Creek Massacre Project
http://www.sandcreek.org
This site includes a history and timeline of the Sand Creek Massacre and information about the Northern Cheyenne Sand Creek Massacre Project.

INDEX

Absarokes (Crows), 34, 36–37, 64; alcohol and, 66; ceremonies, 38, 44, 47, 48–49; clothing, 48; marriage, 39–40; wars, 38, 40–41, 42–43, 46, 47, 48; women, 38, 39, 40, 48

African Americans, 6, 10, 19, 94

alcohol, 29, 66–67, 88

American Fur Company, 41, 53

animals, 11; bears, 29; beavers, 16, 21, 22, 55; bison, 24–25, 55, 67; game, 24, 73; pack animals, 17, 63. *See also* horses

Arapooish (Rotten Belly), 44–45

Arkansas River, 68, 94

Army, U.S., 14, 57, 58, 60, 70, 92–97

Ashley, William, 16, 20, 23, 28, 30–31, 52; wealth of, 29, 30

Battle of Cahuenga, 70

Beckwourth, James Pierson: accomplishments of, 6–7, 50, 101; appearance of, 80, 86; in army, 57, 58–63, 70, 71–73, 90, 99; autobiography of, 6–7, 84, 99, 100; blacksmith, 12–13; chief, 38–39, 45, 46; childhood of, 8–13; children of, 50, 89, 90; with the Crow, 34, 36–55, 100; death, 100; dispatch rider, 71–72, 73; gambler, 76, 77; hotel owner, 71–72; hunter, 14, 24, 73; languages of, 39, 82; legacy of, 101; mail carrier, 74–76; names of, 10, 36, 39, 45, 46; prospector, 76, 77; race of, 6, 10, 65, 94; ranch life of, 82–84, 85; romances and wives of, 12, 30, 39–40, 48, 51, 52–53, 68, 70–71, 88–89, 90, 92; storekeeper, 68, 76, 87; storyteller, 6–7, 18–19, 35, 77, 80, 82, 83–84; trader, 41, 64–68, 69; trapper, 21–23, 25–27, 34–35, 98; view of Native Americans, 6, 14, 43–44, 68, 87, 88, 95, 97

Beckwith, Jennings (father), 8, 10–11, 13, 15, 16, 29; death, 51

Beckwourth, Julia (daughter), 89

Beckwourth, Lou (sister), 51

Beckwourth Pass, 6, 80, 81–82, 101

Bent, William, 65–66

Big Bowl (Crow father), 37, 50

Big Phil the Cannibal, 87–88

Black Kettle, Chief, 94, 96

Black Panther (son), 50

Bonner, T. D., 84, 100

Bridger, Jim, 7, 34, 36, 89, 99

Byers, William, 86, 87

Casner, George, 12–13

Cavalry, U.S., 92, 95–97

Chivington, John, 93, 94, 95, 97

Civil War, 89–90, 92, 94

clothing, 17, 48, 51

Coa-coo-chee (Wild Cat), 60–61

conflicts, Native American and settlers, 9, 11, 26, 31, 72, 86, 87–88, 92–97

Coolbrith, Ina, 80

Crow. *See* Absarokes

Dame Shirley, 82

Denver, Colorado, 86, 87, 88, 97

diseases, 11, 14–15, 23, 53–54

Fitzpatrick, Thomas, 41, 51, 52

Florida, 56–57, 59, 62

food, 17, 19, 20, 22, 23

fur trade, 11, 16–17, 20, 25, 28–29, 55

110

Gentry, Richard, 58, 61, 62
gold rush, 73, 74, 75, 76
Green River, 25, 29, 98
Greenwood, Caleb, 34

Harris, Moses (Black Harris), 19–20
horses, 17, 49, 58, 63
horse stealing, 25, 49, 53, 70, 98

Jackson, David E., 30
Jesup, Thomas, 59, 60

La Jeunesse, Baptiste, 25–26, 27, 34
languages, 34, 39, 50
Le Brache, 26, 27
Ledbetter, Elizabeth (wife), 88, 90
Letts, John, 76–77
Long Hair, 42
Los Angeles (Pueblo de Angeles), California, 69–70

Maid of New York, 58
mail system, U.S., 74–75
maps, 27, 62, 69, 81, 98
Marysville, California, 79, 80, 81
Massacre, Sand Creek, 94–97, 102
massacre, Taos, New Mexico, 72
Mexican-American War, 70–73
Mexico, 69
Micheltorena, Manuel, 70
Missouri Volunteers, 58, 60, 61, 62
mountain men, 6, 16–19, 21, 22–24, 28, 65; dangers to, 23; gatherings of, 28–29, 30–31, 32

Native American nations: Apaches, 72–73; Arapahos, 49, 64, 94–97; Blackfeet, 31–33, 42, 47; Cheyennes, 64, 65–66, 67–68, 85–86, 87, 94–97; Fox, 13, 14; Pawnees, 19, 20; Sac, 13, 14; Seminoles, 56–57, 60, 61; Sioux,

64; Snakes, 30. *See also* Absarokes (Crows)
Native Americans, 6, 9–10, 11, 14, 30–31, 64; attacks on settlers, 9, 26, 29, 31–32, 72, 92; ceremonies, 30; disease, 53–55; food, 20, 24; U.S. wars against, 56–57, 60–63, 92–97; wars among, 38, 42–43
New Orleans, 14, 15
Nom-ni-dit-chee (Little Wife) (wife), 48–49, 50, 88

Payne, Bill, 90
Pine Leaf (Bar-chee-am-pe) (wife), 40–41, 52–53, 55, 88

racism, 6, 10, 56, 59–60, 65, 87, 94
Reed, William, 75
rendezvous, mountain men, 28–29, 30–31, 32
Rocky Mountain Fur Company, 16, 30–31, 37, 41
Rocky Mountain News, 86, 87
Rocky Mountains (Rockies), 16, 21, 74; pass through, 78–79, 80, 81–82

Saint Louis, Missouri, 11, 51, 85
Sandeville, Louise (Luisa Sandoval) (wife), 68, 70–71
Seminole Wars, 57–63
settlers, 12, 86; life of, 11; relations with Native Americans, 9–10, 86, 87–88, 92; trip west of, 12, 79–80, 83–84
Sherman, William T., 75–76
shipwreck, 58
Sierra Nevada (mountains), 6, 74
slavery, 6, 16, 56, 94
smallpox, 53–54
Smith, Jack, 96
Smith, Jedediah, 30
Sonora, California, 76
Still Waters (wife), 37

Sublette, Andrew, 64
Sublette, William L., 30, 52,
   57
Sun Dance, 48

Taylor, Zachary, 60, 61, 62
Towne, Charles, 68, 72
trade and trading posts, 11, 29, 32,
   39, 64, 65–69, 87. *See also*
   fur trade
trailblazing, 22–23, 59, 77–78
trapping, 21–22, 25, 34–35,
   98

Truckee River, 79
Vallejo, Maria Antonia,
   75
Vasquez, Louis, 64, 85, 89

War Horse Ranch, 82–84
weather and seasons, 21, 25, 47,
   62, 82
White Antelope (Spotted Antelope),
   95
Willock, David, 72

yellow fever, 14–15

ABOUT THE AUTHOR

Ann S. Manheimer grew up daydreaming in Los Angeles, California. When she was little, she loved watching cowboy shows on television. As an adult, she has learned that the truth is far more dramatic and inspiring. Manheimer worked as a journalist and a lawyer before settling down to write, teach, and live in the hills overlooking San Francisco Bay. She shares her life with her spouse, two daughters, and two black cats.

PHOTO ACKNOWLEDGMENTS

The images in this book are used with the permission of: © Bettmann/CORBIS, pp. 2, 15, 31, 75; © North Wind Picture Archives, pp. 9, 12, 18, 35, 66, 96; Library of Congress, pp. 17 (LC-USZ62-2034), 57 (LC-USZC4-2398), 71 (LC-USZC4-2957); The Granger Collection, New York, p. 22; Laura Westlund, pp. 27, 62, 81, 98; Courtesy, Colorado Historical Society/William Henry Jackson (CHS.J2462) p. 29; © Todd Strand/Independent Picture Service, pp. 37, 40, 43, 45, 49, 78, 86, 100; American Museum of Natural History, p. 54; Florida State Archives/Florida Photographic Collection, p. 61; Courtesy of the Women's University Club of L.A./Library of Congress, Map Collections, p. 69; © Ann S. Manheimer, p. 83; © MPI/Getty Images, p. 93.

Cover: © Bettmann/CORBIS. Back cover: © Todd Strand/Independent Picture Service.